THE
Wonderful World
of
Wall Street

Where Ordinary People
Can Become Quiet Millionaires

Milton Fisher

Wildcat Publishing Company, Inc.

The Wonderful World of Wall Street
Copyright © 1998 by Milton Fisher

This publication is designed to provide accurate and authoritative information in regard to the subject matter covered. It is sold with the understanding that the publisher is not engaged in rendering legal, accounting or other professional service. If legal advice or other expert assistance is required, the services of a competent professional person should be sought.

From a Declaration of Principles Jointly Adapted by a Committee of the American Bar Association and a Committee of Publishers and Associations

Wildcat Publishing Company, Inc.
P.O. Box 366
Green Farms, Connecticut 06436

First Edition

Book designed by Irwin Wolf

Jacket designed by Gwen Frankfeldt

Library of Congress Cataloging-in-Publication Data

Fisher, Milton.
The wonderful world of Wall Street : where ordinary people can become quiet millionaires / by Milton Fisher.
p. cm.
ISBN 0-941968-10-3
1. Investments—United States. 2. Stock exchanges—United States.
I. Title.
HG4910.F573   1998
332.6'0973—dc21   98-24773
CIP

*This book is dedicated with deep affection and gratitude
to my wonderful wife.*

What Is a Quiet Millionaire?

Thousands of people have become millionaires by playing the market. They have no special skills or training and very little distinguishes them from the millions of others in the market; they become millionaires by thinking for themselves. What they have is "street smarts"—"Wall Street smarts"—a focused honing of several skills in the security markets.

I think of these people as "quiet" millionaires because their fortunes were made without fuss or fanfare. Few people—including friends and relatives—are aware of their success. Many brokers are unaware of how much capital their quiet clients have accumulated, because they use several brokers and they don't trade every day.

Every broker I've questioned about this phenomenon knows that at least one or two of his clients have made it big. I've talked to or dealt with dozens of these success stories, from a Vermont plumber's assistant who calls his broker every day at lunch to a mousy bookkeeper from New Jersey who is worth more than the three partners of the manufacturing firm she works for to a former hot dog vendor from the Lower East Side of Manhattan who finally gave up his wagon to become a registered rep and full-time speculator to a widow with four young children who ran a rooming house until she discovered the market and how it could make her rich to a girdle salesman who was able to save the firm where he worked for twenty-five years by lending it $500,000. The strategies they use reflect their personal idiosyncrasies and thus vary radically. But one characteristic dominates in each case: they keep their own counsel. Don't misunderstand: they listen to their brokers, read financial books and newspaper columns, and watch the TV market shows. When they take action, however, the voice they listen to is their own—and for good reason.

To an overwhelming degree, comments and advice about the market are dished up for professionals, the people who make their living from the complex superstructure known as the market. The talk is always of trends, mass movements, and forces that influence them, that is, interest rates, inflation, the float, federal deficits, taxes. So much of the commentary or discussion is really to provide a reason or excuse for actions to be taken or already taken by people who have to justify their performance. Their advice to a young father or mother with $5,000 to invest is often, "Buy yourself a good CD or a zero coupon bond and come back when you have some real money."

The stock market offers an ocean of opportunity. By the market I mean any kind of security investment—common stocks, preferred stocks, bonds, convertible debentures, warrants, options, commodities futures, calls, puts (see the Glossary for definitions of each). The market offers "fish" for every conceivable size of appetite—whether you "eat" like plankton or like a whale. The quiet millionaires have learned to fish for the less-popular species and found that they are just as nutritious and so much easier to catch.

Most quiet millionaires are investors who have uncovered strategies that get results for them. Those strategies are not necessarily new or unique; they are techniques that have been used with success in the past and will continue to work in the future, but are rarely recommended by brokers. I am pleased to be able to share some of them in this book. Perhaps you will use some of them, or even find your own.

CONTENTS

THE
Wonderful World
of
Wall Street

Part One

Wall Street Smarts

Before you tackle the investment strategies in Part II, you should know some basics. They include learning about the players—those people on Wall Street, like brokers, underwriters, and directors, who provide useful information, good advice, and clues to which strategies to use and when. There are other players who thrive on the seamy side of the Street and, unfortunately, you will no doubt meet some of them as you invest. Perhaps a few words to the wise may help you avoid some of the pitfalls these shady characters put in your path to financial independence.

You will also need a little of the language of Wall Street. Definitions of investment products and procedures may be useful to you and are presented as needed. I've also provided a glossary for a quick review of the terms discussed. The jargon of Wall Street has developed over many years of "insider" (good old boy) activity. Don't worry if you don't know all the terms your broker may throw at you. Ask him to define anything you are not sure of; you may find he doesn't really know the precise definition either. The technical words aren't very important anyway, but understanding the concepts behind them is. This book will help you with the basics every investor should know, but many do not.

Part I also includes a little about how I fell into the world of Wall Street and why it has remained fascinating for me for over fifty years. There are many rewards for the investor on Wall Street—and some of them have to do with what you can learn above and beyond the material things you may achieve. You will enjoy mastering the skills needed to make money on Wall Street, but you will also learn about research and the cutting edge of technology and how the markets fluctuate following world-changing phenomena. Your horizons will broaden as your bank account expands and your freedom increases.

Enjoy the experience.

CHAPTER ONE

Wall Street Is Not a Four-Letter Word

Wall Street was a four-letter word when I was growing up. The depression painted everyone associated with it with a broad brush, and the color was mud. Wall Street caused the devastating crash of 1929. Suddenly we were all poor—dressed in hand-me-downs—discouraged and desperate for a way to survive in a world without jobs, money, or hope. We have all heard about those dark days, and for many years the public generally thought of Wall Street with fear and repugnance.

But after more than three generations of recovery and capitalism, all that has changed. After World War II people began to see Wall Street as a practical way to build personal wealth. By the 1960s it was "in" in a big way, and with the emergence of the baby boomers into middle age in the 1980s, there has never been more money available to invest.

As naïve as this may sound, I woke up to the empowerment of money rather late in life. I was well into my twenties before I realized that money talks. People are so respectful of money. Perhaps more important, money makes a difference in almost every aspect of your life, from filling your most basic needs to your most altruistic dreams.

It's amazing how many young people are so wrapped

up in the pursuit of an education or special training that they fail to realize that there's a limit to how much money they can make by work—even hard, successful work. Very few of us will ever get rich just by working. Yes, there are exceptions, like the great athletes, popular entertainers, transplant doctors, lawyers, and inventors—and those very, very few who make it to the top of the large corporations. But for most hardworking people, a job alone will never move you up the economic ladder. You must put your capital to work.

The surest way to get seed capital is by saving. Saving calls for sacrifice—passing up instant gratification. It is so easy to spend everything you earn—and to charge even more—and thus bury the future! You make so little for all that you do, and there is so much you really need to spend it on. Once you budget for the essentials, however, and a little extra for your kids, it's amazing how little you really need and what you can do without for a while. When you are determined to save, you give up trying to keep up with the Joneses.

Once you set aside your basic emergency fund—usually six months' salary—the rest of your savings should be used to create more capital. Through a thought-out plan—a balance of risk and skill—there is no limit to how far you can go when you put your capital to work. As you acquire investment savings, luck will play a smaller part in your success. Your skill in assessing the risks and rewards ratios in every investment will give you an advantage that will pay off.

Sometimes it happens, when you're struggling up the economic ladder, you can go up one rung and slip down two. Nevertheless, don't get discouraged by losses or investments that don't work out. I've never known a successful investor who didn't acquire his lumps and bruises on the road to success.

After fifty years as an attorney, business advisor, and investor, I am totally convinced that the easiest, safest, and fastest way for the average person to "make it" financially is on Wall Street. Here are my reasons.

Any reasonably intelligent man or woman with a high school education can get all the information needed for success in the market. Every major newspaper has a business section that reports on public companies and the sale and prices of national and local public companies on the New York Stock Exchange (NYSE) and American Stock Exchange (ASE), as well as the National Association of Securities Dealers (NASD) list of over-the-counter stocks (OTC). There are feature stories about the flow of money, taxes, international trade, etc., and one or more financial columnists who comment on current market aspects.

Television and radio provide business news and daily reports. Interviews and panel discussions explain and explore current problems affecting the market. There are TV shows and cable networks devoted to helping you invest. There are also classes, courses, and seminars you can attend. Many brokerage firms offer free breakfast seminars for current and potential customers. Attending any one of these gets you on their mailing list—for life! The large brokerage firms also have books and pamphlets they send to potential customers to explain how the market works.

Perhaps more important, in the last fifty years, there have been thousands of books published about Wall Street that are still relevant. If you really want to learn about the market, there's a cornucopia of information awaiting. Not surprisingly, almost every registered representative (salesperson) is happy to explain and answer the questions of a novice investor.

I remember my first experience. For some months I had been reading and studying the business section of the *New York Times* and absorbing the news and sentiments of various financial sources. It was fascinating to watch the stock prices of companies I recognized, like AT&T, Consolidated Edison, U.S. Steel, go up and down. It gave me a feeling of business sophistication so that I could listen to (and occasionally join in) the conversation of business colleagues without feeling I was in a foreign country. It wasn't long before I realized that many of them had actually made money in the market and, amazingly, didn't seem much smarter than I. If they could do it, maybe I could too.

I began to search the stock tables very carefully. What was I looking for? A strong, famous company with a high dividend? A takeover candidate? A stock that might split soon? No, not at all. I was looking for a low-priced stock so that the $600 my wife and I had saved would buy as many shares as possible. It was clear to me that even a small move, multiplied by many shares, would make a bigger profit than a large move for just a few shares. So I looked for something under $5, and was thrilled finally to find the impressive-sounding General Consolidated Utilities Company, trading at $1 a share. I checked it for two weeks; it went up $1/8$ then back to $1. Then on a Monday it slowed to $3/4$. I watched it, and by Wednesday it was $1/2$, and on Friday it had dropped to $1/4$. So I made my move. I was going to buy two thousand shares—that would be $500. And if it moved up only $1/4$, I'd double my money!

With a bank check drawn on our joint account in my breast pocket, I sat down at a broker's desk. During the past month, I had asked him for quotes from time to time. He was very gracious and friendly, and I was happy that now I could give him some business. I opened an account. Then I told him I wanted to buy two thousand shares of General Consolidated Utilities at $1/4$. He seemed quite surprised and asked me why. I explained my theory and, with a touch of triumph in my voice, ended with, "It's a lot easier for stock selling for $1/4$ to double or triple than for one selling at $50."

He burst into a grin, and then with a giggle he settled

down, apologized for laughing, and explained in a fatherly manner, "This isn't a stock; it's a warrant. See the little 'w' after the name? It gives you the right to buy a share of General Consolidated Utilities preferred stock at $25 per share. Two thousand shares would be $50,000, and, unfortunately, that right to buy expires on Monday. That's why it was dropping so sharply this week—it's all over today."

I was stunned, and unconsciously reached into my pocket to see if the check was still there. It was, and I had learned a mighty important lesson. We chatted for a while, and he made several suggestions for me to check out on my own. My first venture into Wall Street—chilling but instructive.

I had learned the most valuable lesson of my adult life that day: the vital need to ask the question WHY? Albert Einstein once said it is more important to ask the right question than to know the answer. As the price of the stock kept dropping, I should have asked "Why?" instead of dreaming about the profit I could make. Getting the answer to my "why?" would have made my course of action self-evident. Of course, knowing why certain events occur, or why people act as they do, can be the "Open Sesame" to making money anywhere, but it's a lot faster on Wall Street.

It was over thirty-nine years ago that I became more than a casual investor. As a young attorney with a motley clientele of small businessmen and women, I became privy to the problems and challenges of entrepreneurs and the need to put capital to work. One of my clients was particularly enterprising; I was constantly surprised by the deals he got into. One day I was totally surprised when he suggested that he and I become stockbrokers. I had made a few trades and investments, but I was still a novice. He had a little more experience, but, more important, he had a cousin who was a registered representative with a member firm on the New York Stock Exchange.

"What makes you think we could become brokers?" I asked.

"It's a good business, and I don't know anything that compares with it. Here, let me show you. I'm talking about being a broker-dealer in the OTC market—not a member of the New York Stock Exchange or the American Stock Exchange. You know, there are over fifty thousand public companies in the United States, and only about three thousand are listed on the New York or American Exchanges. The broker-dealers trade with each other. They list the companies they make markets in the 'pink sheets,' and advertise what prices they will buy and sell at."

At this point he paused and pulled a sheath of pink sheets with tables of bid and asked prices for hundreds of companies. "Take a look at this," he said and pointed to a company listed as Uranium Mines. There were four brokers who made a market in the stock. Each bid $3^1/_2$ and asked 4. That meant that, if you wanted to sell, they would pay you $3.50, and if you wanted to buy, you'd pay them $4.

"Do you know what that means?" he continued. "If you only made three trades a week, that would be $150, more than enough to pay for the overhead. All the rest would be gravy. Think of what we could do in this business!"

What we didn't know was that the over-the-counter market was as treacherous as a swamp. Bid and asked prices are an illusion—actually only an invitation to trade. One side of the market is regularly soft: if the market makers need stock, they are willing to pay more than the bid price; and if they are anxious to sell, they sell for less than the asked price. So the true margins fluctuate all the time.

Competition forces competitive prices, and the great danger is falling behind the direction the market is going. If you're not careful, you end up with an inventory of stock that you can only sell at a loss—if at all. It can also go the other way: you may keep selling stock that you assume you can replace at low prices, only to find there is none to buy without a loss. You may find that your competition is short of inventory too, and you will be bidding against each other to buy the stock at higher and higher prices.

We joined as partners and soon learned that the lessons of Wall Street are never presented in a nice, orderly fashion. Experience rushes at you, knocks you down, pummels you, kicks you when you are down, and leaves you muttering, "What was that? What happened?" The hurly-burly of every day on Wall Street has lessons for those who take the trouble to learn them. If you don't ask "why?" or "how come?" you're a good candidate for another beating.

CHAPTER TWO

Get to Know the Players

Sometime in 1959, I got a wonderful opportunity to find out about the market and, even more important, to start building a network on the Street. A friend mentioned that he was having dinner with some friends at Wall Street's famous Cavanagh's Restaurant that night.

"Can I come along?" I asked.

"Why not—you'll meet a bunch of great guys, and the interesting thing is they're all making a living on Wall Street," my friend volunteered.

That evening was a revelation. They were friendly and intrigued that a lawyer would be interested in getting into the market. They all spoke freely and were very helpful when I asked each in turn what he did. Amazingly, no two did the same thing and, by and large, were not very knowledgeable about the others' areas of work.

There was Tony, a rather nervous young man who was a trader in an OTC firm. He had originally worked for a member house in charge of OTC trades, but now he was a trader and made markets in about twenty stocks. He reeled them off; it sounded like an auctioneer's spiel. He sat at a trader's desk all day with a telephone headset hooked to many telephone lines and gave quotes on his stocks. The caller had to identify himself before he'd get a quote. Then if a trade were made, a confirmation slip was created immediately with the details of the trade, the name of the trading firm and stockbroker, the number of shares, the time, date, and the price.

When I asked him which stock was safest, or which had the best change for growth, he shrugged his shoulders and said, "I haven't a clue. Each stock is only a number. I don't even know what most of them do. I concentrate on my position and try to figure out what the trend is for each stock. You know, every stock can have a life of its own, regardless of how the rest of the market is going. One of my numbers can double in a day, even though the Dow-Jones is cracking. The key to staying alive is not to get too short or too long. The best deal for me is when there's plenty of action on both sides—you know, buying and selling. An eighth or a quarter on a trade can add up if you've got the volume."

The chap on my left, Stan, was a little older than the rest and sold mutual funds. He had been an insurance salesman for many years and had made a fair but unspectacular living. Then he tried selling mutual funds on the side and soon realized he had been growing the wrong crop. He switched to mutual funds full time and moved up the economic ladder. He found that the economic level of his customers was about the same as those to whom he sold insurance; however, they enthusiastically committed more money to mutual funds than they ever would have to insurance. His customers thought mutual funds were a kind of savings for retirement, which their family might enjoy. This, along with the fun of checking the price on the financial pages and the status of "being in the market," made mutual funds a much easier sale. In those days funds were the "in" thing for young and middle-aged investors, as they were perceived to be safe with a big payoff over time. By having professional investors build a portfolio of many companies, you were protected against being wiped out by the collapse of a few stocks you might have bought yourself. And there were always charts and tables to show you how dramatically money invested in the fund had grown over five, ten, twenty, or even thirty years. Very impressive for the steady, long-term savers.

Stan added, somewhat sheepishly, "I really don't know much about the companies in the fund, but I guess they must be good—the guys who pick them are professionals."

Mike, who sat alongside Stan, laughed. "Say, I guess I'm what you mean when you say a professional. I'm an analyst. My job is to check and follow a company closely. You know, quarterly results, new products, share of market, changes of personnel, new regulations by the state or fed, forecasting earnings, and so on. But I never do the buying or selling. I just pass the information on, and someone else makes the decisions."

"Say, what do you think about IBM right now?" I asked the analyst.

"I haven't the foggiest," Mike said. "I only cover airlines, and I really specialize in just two or three companies—even that's overwhelming. I turn out reports and updates every month, which are passed on to the institutional investors."

No great insights about Wall Street here, I thought, and turned and inquired of Herb, who was sitting at the head of the table and to whom everyone seemed somewhat deferential, "What do you do?"

"Well, I'm a syndicate manager. Do you know what 'new issues' are? That's when a company goes public, and it's the first time the public has a chance to buy an interest in the company. To make sure the money the company wants is raised, it's usually set up so that the first buyers get a good deal. The public knows this and puts in orders for the stock. Very often the orders are for more than two or three times the number of shares available, so when the stock starts to trade, the demand drives the price up—20% or 50% or even 100% over the offering price—making it very tempting for some of those who have the stock to sell. There are also the 'free riders,' hustlers who get the stock and dump it right after the opening. This often results in a sharp drop in the stock price and a very volatile market. It can also cause a negative attitude toward the company. My job is to see that the stock is widely distributed in strong hands who are interested in the future of the company rather than in the immediate price of the stock. That's why we screen the 'expression of interest' when we allot the stock. We try to weed out the 'fast-buck boys.'

"I try to avoid placing the whole issue ourselves and usually form a 'syndicate' of other investment firms to help make a wider distribution, hoping they take the same pains in distribution that I do. It's a tricky operation, full of risks, with opportunities for fraud and disaster. The SEC is right on top of us, but syndicates are the linchpin of public participation in the capitalist system. New issues give an individual a chance to get a piece of the action and the company a chance to get wider recognition and respect and, at the same time, to raise capital relatively inexpensively. It's the most glamorous part of Wall Street, and the most talked about."

"Boy, you can say that again," said Bob, the next diner. "My job is dull, dull, dull, and nobody knows or wants to know what we do. I'm a back-office man, and we have a pretty good crew working back there, but sometimes there's not enough help. We do all the paperwork—get out the confirmations, receive the stock certificates, have them transferred into the correct accounts, check the money, balance the accounts, and try to cope with the mountain of detailed paperwork within the five-day period for settling trades. A hang-up in any area can cause a bottleneck that can take weeks to unravel. And sometimes it doesn't even start in our firm. Suppose some transfer agent can't do his job. He doesn't process the exchange and issue of stock certificates. The domino effect can mess up dozens of firms. It all seems so simple; you get the money from the customer and deliver the stock—baloney! It's a crisis every day I show up for work. Why do I do it? Well, the money is good, and the whole Street is exciting. Every once in a while I hear something and take a flier. There are even times when I hit. Besides, when there's a really good year, you get a piece of the pie. One year I got a bonus equal to a whole year's pay!"

The next man to pick up the conversation was John, a young Harvard MBA, who agreed, "Yes, there's an underlying sense of excitement when you work with money, particularly big money. I'm an institutional rep. It's my job to promote and coddle the people who manage large institutional money, that is, banks, insurance companies, pension funds, union funds, etc. They're very sophisticated investors who have very specific goals. Their performance is closely watched and evaluated almost every month, and for sure, every quarter. The managed money is broken into three groups: equity funds (common stock); bonds (municipal and corporate); and cash (or its equivalent). The percentage in each group varies with the times, or at least with what they think the trends are.

"The job of the institutional investor is to bring in the highest return with the least risk. The greatest sin is to lose money or jeopardize their fund's capital. If they keep it all in cash, they take no risk, but that makes no money. Bonds give them a return, but there is some risk; the bonds can be defaulted, or a change in interest upward can cause the value of the bond's yield to go down. The greatest potential for returns can come from equities—common stock— through high dividends or appreciation of the stock price. But this is also where the greatest risk lies. When the future looks good, they put more institutional money into equities. When there are dark clouds in the economy, the shift is into bonds and cash.

"I keep the institutional investors up to date on what we have for sale—what our analyst thinks. I furnish them with updates on stocks or bonds they already own and on new securities we think are good. They're our bread and butter, and we lean over backwards to keep them happy. Part of my job is to go to all the sporting events, plays, concerts, operas, etc. Of course, I'm not alone. It would be no fun without a money manager or two! My job: keep the buyers happy. Sounds great? It can be an awful drag. Every time there's a little rumble on the Street I have to hold hands with a dozen money managers and come up with explanations and comforting words that they can use with their bosses. Oh well, it's a living! Sure, the more I sell, the more I make, but they have long memories, and the competition is always lurking if you screw up."

"Aw, that's true with all customers," George added. He was in his thirties, a college graduate who had majored in economics and then found out after graduation that there was no shortage of economists. Luckily, he got a job with one of the big brokerage firms. He was given an intensive training course, passed the SEC examinations, and was certified as a registered rep. George explained, "My job is to act as the customer's friend, financial advisor, and general guru. I execute his orders, give him quotes, and try to get any special information he may want, like an annual statement or a copy of the 10K filing by analysts on any companies in which he's interested. But most of all, I try to guide his financial activity. I recommend special situations and try to stop any stupid moves he might be tempted to make.

"The customers always forget your winners, but they never forget your losers, so I'm pretty conservative, and my advice is tempered by who the customer is. A widow living on a pension and savings is very different from the experienced business woman, spreading her capital risks and looking for excitement. It's a lot of responsibility, and many of my colleagues are only interested in having frequent 'traders' for customers. That's where the quick commissions are, but for the long pull, I'm trying to build a base of loyal clients who will stick with me through the years. As they get rich, so will I. Many of my customers become personal friends. You'd be surprised at how many of their secrets I share. Once you're intimate about money, it spreads to other things. Some clients are more knowledgeable about the market than I, and I've learned from their experience."

The last fellow at the table was rather short and slight. He spoke with a touch of an accent—Austrian, I later learned. Very quiet and soft-spoken, Carl had everyone's attention when he said, "I'm an arbitrageur. I try to find situations where you can't lose. Someday I hope to work for myself, but it takes huge capital to make it worthwhile, so I work for a firm that devotes part of its capital to arbitrage, and I run the department.

"Let me give you an example. Suppose General Motors is trading at $50 in volume in New York, and I can buy it in London for $49\frac{3}{4}. By buying and selling at the same time, I can clear $\frac{1}{4}$ point, less the cost of the transaction. But this cannot last long. The competitive market quickly corrects any aberrations that crop up.

"A somewhat more sophisticated example: Suppose the 'A' corporation makes a tender offer for all of the stock of the 'B' corporation at $30 per share. 'B' stock is currently trading at 28, having already jumped 1 point. The market price is still below $30, because there is always the risk that the deal may not go through after the announcement. Believing that the deal will be completed, I carefully begin to buy the stock at 28 or less, so I don't run the price up. If I get nervous about the deal, I might buy 'puts' at $28 for a cost of $\frac{1}{4}$. If the deal breaks, I can get out at $28 with a small loss. But, of course, I'll make less profit if the deal goes through, because of the additional cost of the 'put.' We arbitrageurs would rather make less, but sure."

Since that memorable dinner, I've met scores of men and women who make their living on Wall Street, each engaged in some tiny facet of the great picture. It is interesting to note that there wasn't a single woman at that dinner many years ago. Today I'm sure at least a third of the group would be women.

CHAPTER THREE

Brokers

One of the most important elements in Wall Street success is the selection of a broker. Your broker is in a position to bring you joy or grief—regardless of how sophisticated or knowledgeable you are about the market. It's easy to understand the broker's influence when the client is naïve or just learning about investments: the broker is the client's prime source of knowledge and strategy. Even when the client is a seasoned investor, though, the broker is important because there are times in the course of managing investments when the pros and cons on whether to buy, hold, or sell almost balance one another. The broker's advice often becomes the deciding factor.

Therefore, you should choose your broker with great care. The relationship is as personal as that of attorney and client or doctor and patient, maybe more so, since some investors talk to their brokers almost every day. When we share personal and private information, as well as our dreams and goals, with a broker, that person has a great influence on our life. Your prime criterion for selection should therefore be whether you can trust him or her. This cannot be determined by looking at the firm the broker is with or the clothes he wears or the schools she attended. And it can't be decided in a fifteen-minute interview. With time and experience you should be able to decide whether this is the right broker for you.

You must also find out whether you're on the same wavelength. Is his standard for risk and reward the same as yours? Is she a cockeyed optimist or a doomsday pessimist? Is he really smart enough to be entrusted with your financial future? Is she primarily concerned with your welfare or essentially motivated to generate commissions?

It's not easy to get the answers to these and dozens of other questions about brokers. That's why I recommend using more than one. Incidentally, the individual broker is your financial guy or gal—not the firm. The person, the one you talk with every day, is your guide and guru. He knows about your financial problems and your family. He's part of your life and on your team. To the firm you are just a number in the computer. If your broker changes employers, you will probably follow, as a moving broker takes your entire investment history with him or her as well as your financial philosophy and attitude. No training or exploratory period with a new broker is required, and no one has to be broken in to your investment philosophy.

It's interesting to note, however, that often the change in firm comes about not because the new firm has better research analysts or a better underwriting department, for example, but because the broker is given a bonus, special commission arrangements, or even cash up front for switching firms. The size of the bonus depends on the size and activity of the accounts that are willing to transfer with the broker. I've been sold half a dozen times, but usually I haven't minded because I knew that my broker had my welfare as his priority, not his commissions or the firm he worked for. A good broker knows full well that his clients are his strongest assets, and he nurtures and protects them.

Sometimes it takes years before you realize that "Mr. X" is the wrong broker for you, and so having two or three brokers gives you the comfort of knowing you can drop one or two without any pain. Actually, having several brokers gives you a way to check on their advice. It's amazing how often you will get distinctly opposing answers to the same questions. After a while it's easy to see who knows what he's talking about, on which subjects, and whose guidance you should follow.

It's also an advantage to compare commissions—fees and service charges, which vary among brokerage firms. There are no longer fixed or regulated commission fees; each firm can set its own fees. A broker will always refer to the "regular fee schedule" and then negotiate a percentage discount for you. Almost anyone can negotiate a 25% discount, but there are many who get as much as 50% off.

Through the years, I've probably used a dozen brokers and dropped a few; some have retired or were merged out of existence. I believe learned something from every experience and change, however. Here's one example. About twenty-five years ago I opened an account with a very prestigious old-line firm, when a young man took the trouble to call and set up an appointment at my office to solicit my business. He told me that one of his customers had suggested that he contact me. After an intensive discussion about the market and ways to make money, I came to the conclusion that he was very bright and we seemed to have a compatible outlook on investing. I opened an account and over the years made small purchases on his recommendation. They were profitable, but, more important, he executed my trades promptly and efficiently. He quickly understood the kind of stocks I was attracted to and brought likely candidates to my attention. He didn't push or try to hype me.

One day he was gone, moved to a famous, glitzy, aggressive firm with high-powered salesmen. He asked me to transfer my account to his new firm. I declined, but said I'd be glad to open another account in the new firm with him. I soon noticed a personality change in my broker. He became more aggressive in his recommendations and quite challenging when I declined to act on them. He was also insistent on my trading in larger quantities, His manner was disquieting, but we had been together for a while, and I assumed it was for my benefit.

At home one day packing for a business trip, I got a call from him urging me to buy a thousand shares of Goodyear Tire. In nearly a whisper he explained that the firm had bought a "piece" and was splitting it up among special customers, but only in one thousand or more share lots.

"What do you mean by a piece?" I asked.

"It's a very large quantity of stock at a special price; it could never be accumulated at that price if it were bought piecemeal. You're getting it on the ground floor. It's a prominent company on the New York Stock Exchange and it's going to move. Do it; you'll never get a chance like this again."

"Well, I don't have enough money in my account to cover it, and I'm leaving tonight for a week."

"Forget it, just wire me part of the money. Your account is set up for margin."

"I'll see what I can do."

"No, this can't wait. Yes or no!"

"Okay, I'll take a chance. Buy it."

I got the money by cleaning out all the cash I had. After wiring the money I spent an agonizing week on the road worrying. It was the largest trade in dollars I had ever made and represented a major commitment of my capital. Needless to say, I checked the price of Goodyear every day. Happily, it had moved up a bit by the time I got back to my office.

When I talked to my broker again, I asked him, "Boy, how big was that piece you told me about?"

He didn't know what I was talking about. His fumbling answers made me realize there never had been a "piece." It was all part of a hype, a technique used by this firm to promote sales and to get customers to deal in larger trades and commissions. My nice broker had turned into a barracuda. My welfare was no longer his priority; his commission, or the pressure from his management, was.

I transferred my account to one of the more reliable though less sophisticated brokers I used, and then I sold the stock. If you can't trust a broker, don't do business with him.

Because I did not transfer my account from the original firm, I was notified by mail that John X would be handling my account. A secretary called later and asked me to hold for John X, who introduced himself very briefly as my broker.

Two days later I got an envelope thick with newspaper and magazine clippings about John X. He had been chosen "Broker of the Year" for two years; his annual commissions exceeded $500,000, and a list of famous businesspeople who were his clients was enclosed. I found it very interesting but did nothing.

A week later I got a call from John X himself. "Did you get my clippings?" he asked.

"Yes."

"Don't you want me to be your broker?"

"Frankly, no. I'm not interested in being represented by a "broker of the year" with millionaire clients. Where would I rate in the scheme of things? Surely, I would not be a very important account. I want a broker who needs my business and treats me accordingly."

John X was nonplussed for a moment, but he launched into an impassioned pitch and finally convinced me to try him. I did, and in a few months realized that my first impression was correct—I was just a run of the mill client, and almost all my conversations were with his assistant. I transferred my account to a newlywed with an MBA who was just starting out as a broker.

CHAPTER FOUR

Underwriters and Their Ways

In a firm-commitment underwriting, the theory is that the "underwriter" (someone who undertakes to sell and distribute stock to the public) buys the stock and forms a syndicate of underwriters to help and they resell and distribute the stock to the public. I say "theory" because every underwriting contract contains a "market out clause," which permits the underwriter to get out of the deal if the market turns bad.

The underwriter is understandably concerned about the offering's being priced out of the market (i.e., too high). If the underwriter can't resell, she has to eat (keep) the stock—creating underwriter's indigestion! They hate this.

When a stock opens "soft" (i.e., drops below the offering price), there are some buyers who will take advantage of the rule that the buyer must be furnished with a copy of the final prospectus. After studying it, they have the right to reject the "confirmation of purchase." The odds of ever getting stock in any other "new issue" from that underwriter drops precipitously, as the underwriter does not want to risk having to eat the next stock from the same "shopper" again.

To avoid an onslaught of rejected sales, there is often a "syndicate bid," which provides a floor for the price of the stock until the time expires for rejecting the confirmation. This bid is usually the offering price with an offer to sell at

$1/4$ or $3/8$ of a point above. When the syndicate bid is hit and the shares involved can be traced to the registered representative who made the sale, the commission may be forfeited and the broker may be reprimanded for making a poor sale. To provide some stability to the market, the underwriter is permitted to—and often does—oversell the number of shares he has for sale. In effect he ends up short.

When the "free riders" dump their stock, it reduces the underwriter's oversold position. A "free rider" is someone who sells his stock before he has to pay for it. His plan is to make profit by quickly "flipping" the stock if it opens above the offering price. The broker gets his commission on the buy and sell, even if the "free rider" never spent a penny to "buy" the stock.

So when a company wants to go public, its inflated sense of worth—or greed—must be tempered. The objective is to get the job done, raise the capital, and have a public market for the stock. It would be disastrous to overprice the stock, be unable to sell it, and waste the whole effort, particularly since important money is spent on getting the deal to this point—money for preparing the financials, printing the prospectus, professional fees, filing fees with the SEC, etc. The money spent is important inasmuch as the company needs more—that's why it's going public!

The smarter, surer and safer way to go is to underprice the original offering. Give the public a bargain; make the stock irresistible. There is a powerful reason for the underwriter to be interested in underpricing rather than overpricing. He earns his "spread" only when the stock is sold. No sale, no commission. The higher the price, the greater the commission, sure, but lowering the price affects only a fraction of the commission. Eight percent on a $10 stock is $0.80; on a $9 stock it is $0.72—a lot better than zero. The objective is to make the underwriter's job easier to do. Once the stock starts to trade, many would-be buyers who didn't get any of the initial stock will decide to pay a little more and so move the price of the stock up—probably higher than could have been achieved as an original offering price.

This is all to the good for the company and the insiders. When a company first goes public, only a fraction of its equity is sold to the public. The great majority of the shares remain with the insiders (founders, limited partners, venture capitalists, management/owners, etc.). The price at which the stock trades reflects the value of the stock they own, and so when they want to borrow against the stock or sell it, there will be some measure of its worth.

A successful underwriting enhances the value of the company itself by giving it a good name with the investing public and promises of a source for future creation of capital. It makes the company a better credit risk for banks and other lenders. It also lays the foundation for growth of the company. With a strong price for the stock and an active market, a successful underwriting makes it easier to acquire other companies for stock rather than cash and also to attract talent with stock options or stock as a lure.

It is in the business of new issues, however, that you find the most outrageous and greedy behavior by some of the largest and most prestigious underwriting firms. Instead of a fair and widespread distribution of "hot stock" to the public, such stock is often earmarked for a small coterie of individuals and firms who withhold and manipulate it for their mutual advantage. When 50, 75, or even 100% of the entire issue is traded in the first few days, you don't have to be Sherlock Holmes to suspect that the original issue was not widely distributed to public investors, as the law requires: There are probably dozens of ways to avoid the law, and new ones will always be found.

A simple example is how Sandy stumbled into a way to riches in the "new issue" market some years ago. His broker was a big producer in a very active underwriting firm. This broker always put in for a large quota of new issue stock and distributed it among his better clients.

But the new issue market is a sometime thing; it has its own cycles, often independent of the general market. And there are times when the new offerings are not in demand and it's hard to place the stock.

The cycle is very easy to understand: when you have had a long period during which you can't sell initial offerings, the underwriter and companies that want to go public tailor better and better deals for the public. Eventually, they offer a bargain that is so obviously irresistible that it's gobbled up and immediately starts to trade above the offering price. Other underwriters do the same thing, and suddenly there's a hot market—all other new issues go up to a premium and the public wants more. To fill the demand underwriters come up with offerings that are not such great bargains— eventually truly terrible deals for the public—pure gambles.

How does this come about? The potential issuers of new stock don't live in a vacuum. They know there's a hot market. They know it from every side—their lawyers, accountants, key personnel, everyone smells a new issue boom. The would-be underwriters, or their "finders" buzzing around, begin offering the company better terms than the other underwriters are offering, in the hope that they will get to market "before the window closes." Nothing stops them; the public fights to get every deal, the prices rise to greater and greater premiums, until one day, it seems that in the investors' subconscious a whistle is blown and everyone becomes aware that "the emperor has no clothes." All the new issues now are bombs, and you can't give one away.

It was during one of these dry periods that Sandy was importuned by his broker to help him out by buying a few hundred shares of an initial offering. "It's not really a dog, Sandy. It has earnings and some very interesting new products. But for some reason nobody is buying. Help me out; take a few.''

Sandy did and, although the price dropped immediately after the syndicate bid was withdrawn, the stock eventually turned around, and within a year Sandy was able to get out with a small profit. When the next phase of the new issue cycle arrived and the market was beginning to heat up, Sandy was out in front for a few hundred shares of a new company that went for a premium.

Soon Sandy was saying, "Why can't you give me more shares? Remember, I helped you."

"I'd love to, but I have to spread it among my better customers. After all, they provide me with the day-to-day bread and butter business. Besides, Sandy, you're making a terrific return on your money on the stock I do give you. Hold them, you'll get terrific premiums."

"The heck with holding them, I don't want to take the chance. I've been there before. I've had hot stock that was up 50%, held because it was supposed to be so good and would go higher, and then finally sold at a loss! I'll take a sure profit every time."

"Okay, Sandy, tell you what I'll try. I'm going to give you a much higher allotment, but you must sell it the first few days, even though you think the price is going higher."

Sandy says, "You've got a deal, and, what's more, you can sell me out anytime you want. I'm not greedy. I just want a sure profit."

And that's the way it went. The broker made at least three commissions on every block of new issue stock he confirmed to Sandy: one on the buy, one on the sale, and then another when he crossed the stock by selling to another of his customers who couldn't get all the stock he wanted at the opening price.

The broker's pitch was: "It's a hot deal. I'll try to get

you some stock if you'll take a like amount in the after market."

"Sure, why not," says the second customer, "I'll still be getting stock that averages less than the opening price."

Ultimately, the broker makes a fourth commission when that stock is sold. No wonder some brokers love new issues.

Sandy did extremely well when there was a hot market: the allotment grew bigger because the scheme worked and there was no risk. He never argued about the commissions. The only cloud was his awareness that the raging market wouldn't go on forever. The silver lining, however, was that the new issue cycle repeats itself every few years. And Sandy and his friendly broker could always make other investments.

If it seems outrageous and illegal, that's because it is! But people get away with it, and the saddest and most frustrating part is that this is the tale of only one small registered rep. The same kinds of flimflamming deals are the stock in trade of some of the most prestigious firms in new issues.

Initial offerings are, nevertheless, an excellent way to make money in the market—not in the "hot issue" phase of the cycle but after there has been a bust and a long dry period. The deals that are brought out then are those that result from long, hard pursuit of reluctant underwriters by companies that need capital badly and are willing to offer better and better terms to the public. Ironically, these good deals don't go to a premium. Often the underwriters can barely sell them, and sometimes they have to eat part of the offered stock.

Eventually, however, the wholesome deals work out. Another advantage is that you can accumulate more stock at a reasonable price, as your judgment is confirmed by the company's performance and before the free market wakes up and brings the price up to what the stock is worth.

CHAPTER FIVE

Directors

One of the great popular illusions about big business is that large corporations are run by the Board of Directors. That has about as much validity as the belief that Great Britain is run by the queen. The Board of Directors looks very impressive on an organization chart. It is positioned so all can see that "the buck stops here" and that all authority and power emanate from the board. This is a great comfort to some stockholders, who believe that the Board of Directors is an impressive group of sophisticated and independent businesspeople watching over the corporation's activities and the stockholders' welfare.

Legally and technically, that's what a board should do, but like Gershwin tells us, "it ain't necessarily so." Most boards are dominated and by a single individual or a small group of directors who set the board's agenda and policies and thus influence the operation of the whole corporation. They control the election of officers and top executives, and they judge performance and the achievement of corporate goals.

Is there any special training, educational requirements, or special experience required to become a director? Not at all! Directors are elected by the stockholders at an annual meeting for a one-year term or, in some companies, for a three-year term.

Shouldn't this be enough to ensure an honest and effective board? in theory—but only in theory. The stockholders are given a list of nominees who are selected by the nominating committee; the nominating committee is selected by the Board of Directors. And remember: the board is dominated or led by one individual or a small group. It is very rare for a director to get elected if he is not one of the controlling interest's nominees. When there is a real election, it's usually because of a fight for control of the corporation. Then the small stockholders get a chance to make a real selection. There are usually two slates representing the two factions fighting for control. You'll get a flurry of letters and pronouncements from each side bombarding you, the independent stockholder, with accusations, recriminations, name-calling. This is often the only time you can find out what's going on behind the corporate shutters.

In many ways it's an unfair battle. Management, that is, the incumbent directors, is able to use corporate money for mailings, telephone calls, professional solicitations, advertisements, public relations—sometimes even radio and TV coverage. The insurgents, as outside challengers, must use their own money, at least until they've won. If they get control, they reimburse themselves! Occasionally, in these wars, some sitting directors join the revolution. This, of course, is the unkindest cut of all to those who have been dominating and directing the board.

You can see now why nominating committees are chosen with such care. Anything other than a rubber stamp could cause a problem. What determines who will be nominated? Nominees are usually a friend or business associate of the leader—someone who is safe, a non-boat-rocker who will go along and vote "yes" when the signal is given, someone whose background is filled with important-sounding titles and experience and who serves elsewhere as a director with "go-along" credentials.

Why would a successful businessperson serve as a director? On the downside, there is some risk. There is exposure to personal liability for each director for gross negligence, but officers and directors liability insurance is paid for by the corporation. As a practical matter, the individual director rarely has to pay anything out of his own pocket; however, the potential unpleasantness and aggravation of being dragged through a lawsuit, tried in the media as well as the courts, is a possibility.

So what is the upside to being a director? Well, there is the prestige of being a director of an important public corporation, a relatively exclusive club not open to 99.9% of the rest of the world. Then there is the money. Directors, who are not employed by the corporation, may earn basic compensation—often $25,000 or higher per year—plus $1,000 or more for each board meeting attended, and additional fees for appearing at each committee meeting. There are also all-expense-paid trips to inspect corporate facilities or due-diligence assignments covering potential acquisitions or mergers, and, of course, pensions and severance compensation.

The trend today is for directors to own some stock in the company. They want to show a financial community of interest with the common stockholders. Many public corporations also provide options for the directors to buy stock at very attractive prices. So-called independent directors are not employees or controlling stockholders; they are essentially "token" stockholders. It's instructive to note the relatively insignificant cumulative percentage of stock held by the directors (except for the dominant one or two who really control the board).

The most important perks of the director's job are more valuable than the financial gain of fees or stock she holds. Directors are happy to keep their "jobs" and perhaps qualify for becoming directors of other corporations. They are also looking for other non-boat-rockers like themselves to serve on the boards of their own companies, those that they may have controlling interest in. It's interesting and somewhat chilling to see the vast pattern of interlocking directorships—the most-exclusive "good old boys" club of the business world—all safe and secure supporters for management. A wonderful study was done on this phenomenon several years ago by William Domhoff. Out of this research came *Who Rules America?* and the sequel, *Who Rules America Now?* Both books show the pattern of interlocking directorships held by Ivy League college classmates, golf club members, summer home neighbors in Maine and Newport, all serving on each other's corporate and nonprofit boards.

This became almost funny several years ago, when boards tried to be responsive to the times and decided to bring women and minorities into the otherwise homogeneous boardroom. They figured one minority woman was the easiest solution, but the good old boys didn't know many. So you now see a few minority women, usually from academia, serving on lots of boards of companies that have nothing to do with their areas of research or knowledge. These women probably know they are being used as token, and they usually serve on the "community relations" committees of these boards, but at least they have gotten a toe in the door. It should be easier for women and minorities to become directors in the future.

Well, then, who is watching out for the humble stockholder? Frankly, no one. The common stockholder must watch out for himself or herself. Most of the time, the stockholder must sit by and watch corporate actions that don't seem quite legitimate. If totally disgusted and frustrated, he or she can always sell the stock and try something else.

That is the beauty of public companies, even small ones.

CHAPTER SIX

A Stockholder's Only Recourse

The Board of Directors often proves useless in preventing the controlling directors or managers from improperly using funds for personal gain, from squandering capital in bad business decisions, from abusing power, or even from committing illegal acts. What can the average stockholder do then? In truth, very little. Negative press might help, and an exposé on *60 Minutes* or *20/20* would certainly bring many boards to their knees. But most stockholders don't have the power of the press behind them.

There are, however, two very important weapons the small stockholder has: the derivative stockholder's suit and the class action suit. Each is rooted in a somewhat different philosophy, but both have the advantage of achieving substantial cash judgments against the corporation, its officers, or directors. Therefore, experienced and sophisticated lawyers will undertake the expense and effort of litigation on a contingency basis. The money recovered for the stockholders may make millions for the lawyers, but there is no cost to the stockholder if they lose.

In the derivative suit the theory is that, as a stockholder, you have the right to sue the officers and/or directors in the name of the corporation for whatever skulduggery is going on, as they would never sue themselves. If the legal action is won, the officers and directors may personally be responsible for the money judgment awarded, and the attorney's fees and expenses are paid from the judgment—from the individuals, officers, or directors, or, more realistically, from the insurance company.

A class action suit is brought by a large group of people or stockholders who claim to have been wronged. But the amount of damage to each is relatively small; therefore, it does not pay for any individual to sue. One or more persons may start a suit on behalf of the entire class, but they must satisfy the court that they are indeed representative of the class and competent to carry it through. Here again, the lawyers are very important, and their incentive is the potential for big fees. Some examples of class action suits are: the asbestos suits of a few years ago, suits against auto manufacturers or petroleum companies, and the huge class actions against the tobacco companies.

Over the years I've become firmly convinced that only the threat of potential class actions and derivative suits has kept some rapacious and greedy managers from looting our public corporations and eventually destroying the capitalist system. Despite this potential deterrent, there are still thousands of examples each year of management defalcations, embezzlements, theft, diversion of assets, and other corporate shenanigans.

CHAPTER SEVEN

The Seamy Side of the Street

In a small western town the largest saloon was ablaze with light one Saturday night when a stranger walked in, took a drink, danced with two of the girls, and then floated to the backroom and the high-stakes poker game. After observing as few hands, he called for a chair and joined the game. Intent on the cards and the lively betting, he did not pick up on the winks and nods of one of the girls watching the game during the first half hour. Eventually it dawned on him that she wanted to tell him something, and so when she left the room, he asked for the men's room and said he'd be right back. He had no trouble finding her in the dance hall and got the next dance.

"I've been trying to get your attention," she said, "so I could warn you—that poker game is crooked. You could get cleaned out."

"Aw, I know that, honey, but it's nice of you to warn me. Sure it's a crooked game."

"Why do you play then?" she asked.

"Well, honey, let's face it. It's the only game in town."

Wall Street and that story have a lot in common.

When you want money and excitement, there's nothing like Wall Street. It can be the only game in town. Of course, as with any form of gambling, there's also a seamy side. Wall Street attracts every kind of bad character: con artists, short-changers, sharks and slickers, and just plain crooks. They are there for the same reason you are: they want to make money. The difference is, they don't care how. You play by the rules, they don't. You and your money are fair game. In fact, taking you for a ride is the most fun part of their game; it makes the win sweeter.

They don't wear identity badges to indicate that they're the bad guys. They ooze respectability and integrity. Often they have titles, great credentials, fancy offices, and unimpeachable connections. Their great wedge is your gullibility and greed. They're always looking for suckers. And they fish the public like a well-stocked trout pond. They only need a small percentage to make a success.

If you're in the market, you must recognize that this is part and parcel of Wall Street, one of the hazards of this moneymaking merry-go-round. It's a rare week indeed that the business pages do not report some new Wall Street scandal or scam. Note well: when you open an account with a broker and you sign an authorization form, often you've also agreed to submit any disputes and disagreements to arbitration instead of litigation. The reason given is that it's so much faster and cheaper to solve problems through arbitration with people who understand Wall Street. But "it ain't necessarily so!" NASD arbitrators awarded $41 million in 1995 for damages. Just image the number of times guilty firms settled before arbitration or before final judgments, the number of times individual brokers settled privately before their managers found out, and, sadly, the number of times the clients never became aware that they had been taken or couldn't afford to fight back.

In one case in 1996, the broker persuaded his client to aggressively buy a sparsely traded stock. His purpose was to keep the price of the stock up while he and his family secretly sold their shares. The client bought 68,000 shares at a cost of about $450,000 while the broker dumped 400,000 shares for about $3.5 million. The client was eventually able to get out with a $250,000 loss. The firm was fined $500,000 in punitive damages, because it was allegedly aware that its employee was selling while recommending that his client buy the stock through another brokerage firm, and the firm did nothing about it.

There are many situations in which it is almost impossible to protect yourself from an unethical broker or firm. For example, there was a time when a highly regarded brokerage firm on the East Coast was paying its obligations with checks drawn on a bank in California. This trick delayed payment for about a week in the 1970s, when interest on money was running at about 18–20%. If the float in checks ran to $100 million, the loss to the payees was about $400,000 to $500,000 per week. Hardly cricket! There was very little individuals could do about it, but a class action suit brought the firm to justice.

In the spring of 1996, the Justice Department investigated a well-known rating service for allegedly improperly pressuring bond issuers to hire them or face negative comments and low bond ratings that would affect the marketability and cost of the bonds to be issued. Just about the same time, the U.S. attorney in Manhattan revealed a sting operation run by the FBI newspaper headlines read "Big F.B.I. Sting Collars 45 Penny Stock Figures." Arrests disclosed the practice whereby individual brokers were paid under the table for promoting and selling stock the firm wanted to unload. It's interesting that the newspapers and magazine accounts of this and similar schemes usually associate the "con" with "small-stock" or "over-the-counter" company securities, but the same kind of thing goes on with companies listed on all the exchanges. The modus operandi, somewhat refined, is used by the most prestigious firms.

The most obvious and widespread example of fraud is in the distribution of initial public offerings, the new issues where the underwriter has control over the number of shares and disposition of all the stock earmarked for public trading. Too often it is delivered in "blocks" to associates or business partners of the underwriter. This is an area begging for attention and investigation by government regulators.

What can you do to protect yourself? Stay on your toes and develop a skeptical, suspicious, and ungullible attitude toward all moneymaking ideas. Treat them like strange food or drink. Before you ingest, examine, test, smell, taste, and only nibble a little before you're sure. If you're told "it's now or never," take "never" every time; there will always be another train leaving the station.

Your broker may be the most dangerous person in your life, this despite the fact that his integrity and loyalty to you may be unquestionable. His gullibility may destroy you when he makes recommendations based on what he believes to be true. A friend of mine took a substantial loss when he followed the advice of one of his brokers, whose integrity he still respects. This broker was conned by his manager, who had told all the salesmen that he had invested his own mother's pension fund in the stock.

Remember, if your broker was so smart, he wouldn't be a broker. He'd be a multimillionaire letting someone else make the commissions while he took the capital gains.

CHAPTER EIGHT

The Language of Wall Street

As a young child, one of my favorite stories was told to me by my father. It concerned a poor tailor who would sit in his open air stall on the fairgrounds and sew for a living. His earnings were meager despite the long hours he put in every day, and he was generally held in very low esteem by the people of the village. Although he was healthy and friendly and always in good spirits, he could not find any woman who would marry him.

Then one day, as he toiled with his needle and thread on a shirt-to-be, he was bedeviled by a swarm of flies. They bit him on the neck and face. His ears were a delicacy; his bare legs became a field to harvest for those brazen flies. Time and again he shooed them away, to no avail. They immediately returned; it was fun to them. Finally, in a moment of sheer exasperation, the young tailor grabbed a towel and brought it down with a bang on his work table. The noise and air current the blow created brought a moment of peace.

As he withdrew the towel, the tailor was stunned to find that he had caught seven flies, which lay crushed on the table. He was overcome with the result. "Seven in one blow," he kept muttering to himself. Filled with the sense that this could only be accomplished by divine intervention, he began to believe that this was a miracle the world should know about. He threw down his apron and set about making a sign he could wear as a sandwich board so that his message could be read from the front or the back. In bold letters it proclaimed, SEVEN IN ONE BLOW! Dressed in his best clothes, with the sign in place, he strode forth with his head held high—fearless and proud of his accomplishment.

The villagers were surprised to see the shy little tailor strutting about, but when they read the words on his sign, they were gripped with awe and respect. Never had they suspected the power and strength of their quiet neighbor. That he could kill seven with one blow was astonishing.

"They must have deserved it," they thought. "He was a good man, the seven were probably thieves and brigands who were trying to rob him. How wonderful that he could destroy those wicked men and with one blow no less!"

The little tailor's story spread like thunder and echoed from the hills. Soon he was a celebrity—everyone wanted to be his friend and to do business with him. In a short time, he became a rich man and, miracle of miracles, he married the king's daughter!

Now, what has all this to do with a book about Wall Street smarts? It points out the great need to know what people mean when they're talking Wall Street talk. The special language of Wall Street can be used to conceal or to confuse, as well as to reveal. Some of the ambiguity is no accident.

Financial accounting should be the foundation of an efficient market. An audited financial statement should give an investor a reliable picture of a company's worth and progress. Unfortunately, the standards and rules followed by public corporations are not completely uniform. Management all too often wants to put a spin on the numbers to manipulate the results and to give the public a certain impression (usually overstated but sometimes understated).

There are two accounting standards that currently affect the financials. The Financial Accounting Standards

Board or FASB makes rules for company financials; these rules must be followed to get an okay from auditors. The FASB continues to develop accounting standards for reporting complex financial problems that will give a better picture of the company's worth. The Generally Accepted Accounting Principles, or GAAP, lay out the standards and rules that have been used by the financial and business community for many years and carry the imprimatur of SEC "acceptable procedures."

Nevertheless, there are still dozens of accounting gimmicks and techniques that can be used to distort a company's value and progress. Many can be unraveled only by a passel of accountants and financial analysts, but others can be understood and evaluated by any intelligent and careful investor. With the widespread use of the P/E ratio as a gauge, earnings per share has grown in importance as an investment guide, so much so that it is included in the stock market tables reported daily by the *New York Times* and the *Wall Street Journal.* How weak a guide it is, though, when special accounting treatment can cause earnings per share to vary so drastically. So when you're digesting a corporation's annual statement, there are some important areas to note in evaluating the earnings per share: Tax loss carry forwards, depreciation, real estate, capital assets, options and convertibles.

Taxes

Does the corporation use or have any special tax treatment? Since the tax on earnings can be almost 50% from the combined federal, state, and city levies, it affects earnings per share drastically. There are also many ways in which the tax burden can be reduced, sometimes for years.

When a corporation has a carry-forward loss, it can shelter and reduce the tax for the years it takes to absorb the loss. The earnings per share of a corporation that pays 50% in taxes should not be valued the same way as for a company that pays no taxes. There are times when a huge carry-forward tax loss is the most important asset a company has. This loss must be used within a certain time frame, however (a maximum of fifteen years). The number of years remaining is detailed in the notes to the balance sheet, and this helps you judge how long the company will have a tax advantage. There are many tax incentives created by the government to motivate business. You should note them when assessing and projecting future earnings per share.

Depreciation

Depreciation is an accounting treatment whereby a company recognizes that some assets do not last forever and most ultimately be replaced; therefore a portion of the stated value is set aside each year to account for deterioration. Depreciation is treated as a cost of doing business and so reduces profit and earnings per share. The percentage used for depreciation for different assets is stated in the "notes to financials" and usually is within GAAP standards.

There are occasions, however, when "depreciation" is used to wipe out a profit, for example, by writing off capital machinery in one year because it is obsolete or no longer used, or because management wants to offset a large capital gain that year, or to reduce taxes to preserve cash.

Real Estate

Real estate can often be a value that is not reflected on the balance sheet. If a company owns important real estate in the form of buildings, manufacturing plants, land, long leases, etc., which were acquired many years ago, the balance sheet may carry them at original cost—despite the fact that today's values may actually be ten times or more higher. The reverse may also be true: the original cost could be one hundred times what it would bring in today's market. This is especially true in depressed areas or with very old factories with major environmental cleanup costs. Knowing what the true picture is can help you make a better evaluation of the company's worth.

Capital Assets

Capital assets consist of machinery, special equipment, production lines, etc., and should be examined like real estate. They are usually stated at cost less the depreciation accumulated; however, their true worth must be considered to get the real picture.

For example, a company that once had to build a railroad connector to deliver its products to the main lines now delivers primarily by truck. It carries that rail line at its original cost less depreciation, although it will never rebuild and could probably only get a pittance for it today. This overstatement of assets, of course, skews the company's net worth upward.

The opposite can apply here too. Capital assets in the form of roads, mines, patents, copyrights, vineyards, orchards, may be stated at the original cost yet currently be worth many times that amount.

Options

In recent years it has become fashionable to provide incentives for key employees and management over and above their salaries. The most widely used device is stock options. The employee is given an option to purchase common stock at a fixed price for a number of years. When the price of the stock increases beyond that fixed price, the employee has the opportunity to exercise the option and to profit handsomely. This is a very effective way of augmenting the compensation package in a competitive labor market. Unfortunately, it has also become a way to enrich managers who control the company. For example, Sanford Weill, CEO of Travelers Group made $96 million in 1996 because of stock options, after he had "downsized" thousands of longtime employees to "increase profits" and earnings per share on paper.

Options have become so important that they must now be reported in the financial statements. The percentage of options given to each individual must be indicated. It is here that you'll often find that the people who control the company get the lion's share of the options. Examination and study of options can be important in assessing corporate worth. It is also a good way to assess whether you want to be associated with a company.

For example, if the common stock is trading at $10 and there are three million shares issued, and if there are options to buy two million shares at $5 per share, the value of the outstanding issued shares will surely be diluted. Earnings per share will change because the profit will be divided by five million shares rather than three million. Of course, the corporation will get $10,000,000 of new capital, which it will put to work.

The problem of the "cost to company" for options is so important that the FASB has been trying for years to adopt a standard whereby the cost to the company would be reflected in the financials and thus reduce profits. The FASB believes that issuing options reduces the present worth of a company and that stockholders and potential investors should know this. Management has expressed considerable opposition to this proposed accounting treatment.

Convertibles

Convertible bonds, preferred stock, or warrants have the same potential for confusion as the options. Once the conversion is made, there is new common stock and a dilution of equity per share. Sometimes, the number of new shares can even exceed 50%—an important factor when trying to project earnings per share for the next five years.

If you hold convertibles, there is another consideration. As the common stock approaches the conversion price, there is an incentive for the company to "call the issue," that is, pay it off before the price of the common stock makes it desirable to convert and dilute the present common stock. This, of course, robs holders of one of the reasons they bought the convertible. Converting also puts off the tax event and preserves the holding time needed for capital gains treatment. Each case must be analyzed on its own and thought through; holders of convertibles shouldn't automatically tender when an issue is "called."

CHAPTER NINE

Trading

Trading is a fantastically complex and emotional activity that sounds simple but is not. The most widespread and inane bit of advice on how to make money is "buy low and sell high"—as if anyone could know what's low or where high is. Lifetimes have been spent learning how to recognize or determine what's low and what's high. But as a practical matter, that's what trading is all about. And Wall Street is about trading—the buying and selling of stocks and bonds and the various derivatives of the financial species.

There are three kinds of trading in the market, and they have to do with time: short-term trading, intermediate trading, and long-term trading

Short-Term Trading

Buy and sell in a few days or weeks, sometimes in and out in a day and even several trades of the same stock in a day—this kind of trading is usually reserved for the professional or someone with great capital reserves who buys and sells millions of dollars in equities throughout the day. The volume makes fractions of a point important. This is not a happy area for the amateur.

There are money managers who will do this for you for a set fee, usually a percentage of your invested portfolio, billed quarterly. Ostensibly, this saves you money if you are a very active trader, since they do not bill for every trade. Unfortunately, you still have to pay them even if they lose money for you in a given period. You can do this kind of trading with less than millions, since money managers are working simultaneously for hundreds of clients. They buy and sell constantly, often using the "puts and calls" strategy, and they inundate you with trade confirmation slips and prospectuses. Because they move so fast, you have very little say about which stocks they buy or sell and when. For all the negative reasons described in the mutual funds chapter (chapter 28), giving up control of your portfolio to play the game this way isn't recommended. This is a growing part of Wall Street, however, and you may get calls from people who do not identify themselves as brokers, but as private money managers or portfolio managers. They are really still brokers looking to be paid in a better, more predictable way— for themselves.

Intermediate Trading

Speculation positions are taken and held for weeks or months in this kind of trading. This time frame is the favorite of many stockbrokers and market players. It offers excellent opportunities for commissions and also is a way for the speculator to build capital in a relatively short time. But it is not a recommended way of trading, and most amateurs do not have the time to analyze many stocks in the relatively short time this type of trading requires.

Long-Term Trading

Investments are held for years or for decades in this type of trading style. This is the kind of investment made by institutions and wealthy individuals—often second-generation stockholders. There is no need for frenetic activity, no demand to show immediate results. You have the time to get to know the companies you invest in and to thoroughly understand how they fit into your investment goals and strategies. The goal is substantial capital appreciation, very few tax implications, and, incidentally, a defense against inflation.

Remember, taxes are an important consideration in all trading decisions. Federal tax laws lowered capital gains taxes to 20% in 1998, for example, so many intermediate and short-term traders may have held longer than usual in 1997. Individuals in high tax brackets sometimes choose to invest in tax-free or tax-deferred products, even when the return is not as attractive as higher yielding but taxable growth securities.

CHAPTER TEN

Annual Statements

A popular assignment in a course I used to teach went like this. The class of thirty adults or so was told that each student would have to have a buddy or partner for the ensuing class session. The process of negotiation and selection of buddies would have to be done in ninety seconds. Students did not have to accept the invitation to be anyone's buddy, but, on the other hand, if someone didn't have a partner within the time limit, he or she had to miss that class session. And you could not select anyone you already knew. I gave them two minutes to look around the room to make mental selections and to plan their strategies. Then the exercise started and pandemonium reigned. Excitement and terror were evident as some students remained in their seats and others rushed around the room looking for a suitable, willing buddy. This was only the beginning of the exercise. The "buddies" were then told they had five minutes to find out as much as they could about each other and then get back to their seats. When they all settled down I called on each of them at random to give a speech about their buddy. It was remarkable how much information some of the buddies had elicited and how little others had garnered. The most important part of the lesson, however, was highlighted by a question after they had finished their speech: "What did you learn about your buddy that he or she didn't tell you?"

This was always a bit of a shock to the speaker and the class: "How could I know something he didn't tell me?" Then they began to realize that they had formed many impressions about their buddy that didn't come from his or her lips: "He's very confident and sure about himself—very strong in all his opinions." Or "She's gentle, kind, and sensitive to other people." Or "He's very ambitious and would probably make a great leader." Or "She has a great sense of humor and really enjoys whatever she does."

How much more important your subjective observations are than the bare facts when you're trying to get a true picture of an individual.

What has all this to do with making money on Wall Street? A great deal! For most of us, there is little likelihood that we will ever meet the CEOs or movers and shakers of a public corporation we might invest in. Yes, we can probably see them at an annual meeting or get most of the hard facts—sales, products, franchises, patents, manufacturing facilities, percentage of market, margin of profits, long-term debt, and so on—from Value Line or Standard & Poor's reports. But statistics are not enough. What can you find out about a company other than the cold, hard facts?

There are vital aspects of a business and its potential that can help you determine whether it's a good investment. What kind of people lead it? Is it run by a dictator? Does it value form over function? Does management act as if it owns the corporation and views the stockholders as a necessary evil? Does management whittle away at stockholders' rights?

These and dozens of other questions can be answered by an intelligent study of the Annual Report (also known as the Annual Statement), the notice of the Annual Meeting, and proxy material enclosed with both in the same mailing. The Annual Statement gives information of interest to customers, banks, competitors, and the public, as well as stockholders. It describes the business (or businesses), its products and markets, and the financials—debt and tax loss carry forwards, profit and loss statement, and balance sheet—usually compared with the same time frame a year ago. It also lists officers, directors, any new and ambitious plans, recent or pending acquisitions, and so on.

The proxy material gives very important information for the alert stockholder: a list of beneficial owners of more than 5% of the common stock and their relationship to management, if any; a minibiography of each of the nominees for the Board of Directors—their backgrounds and compensation option plans; salaries and employment contracts of the top executives; performance graphs; "certain transaction items," which highlight potential conflicts of interest and self-dealing or family control changes; and so on.

Annual statements and proxies are amazingly creative. They range from the simplest bare bones photocopy of the 10K's, which public corporations must file with the SEC, to the most elaborate four-color "books" that compare favorably with the slickest fashion magazines. Close study will be worth your while and help you weed through the slick graphics to the truth of the company's condition. You may even glean some unintended information from annual reports, by reading between the lines:

1. Pictures of the chairman of the board or CEO and quotes from him or her are everywhere, and he or she is the only one given credit for any accomplishment. This is a clue that the chairman or CEO is an egomaniac.

2. The company spent a fortune on an annual report for only three hundred stockholders, despite a losing or a marginal year. Is this an ego thing for the president, or is he or she trying to fool you into thinking things are better than they are? And, of course, it's terribly wasteful.

3. Directors are elected for three-year terms, and staggered elections ensure control by the insiders, who always have a majority on the board, even if there should be a chal-

lenge to the management-endorsed nominees in any one year. This indicates that management is primarily concerned with self-preservation and its aggrandizement at the expense of stockholders.

4. Management constantly increases benefits to insiders, with little or nothing to stockholders. Insiders receive new and more attractive options, such as reducing the option strike price when the price of the common stock has fallen, loans under sweetheart terms, contracts, and business with firms in which the insiders have a large stake. Management acts as though disclosure in the proxy material makes all these cozy deals cricket. And management offer ever-increasing salaries and pension terms, wildly beyond what insiders could get for their services anywhere in the free market. In short, management acts as though the corporation was its personal property, although this group owns relatively very few shares.

5. The proxy statement must list stockholders whose beneficial interest is 5% or more and their relationship to one another. The list and the relationship of officers and directors often make it clear that the corporation is ruled by a monarch who has created a dynasty with a hierarchal system of succession (all his to give, obviously by divine right).

6. If there are new stockholders listed for whom you have knowledge and respect—prominent venture capitalists, mutual funds, or sophisticated entrepreneurs—it could be a good sign. They evidently think the company is okay and will do well. On the other hand, if an important stockholder reduces or sells out her position or leaves the board, you should wonder why. Changes in the list of beneficial owners and the number of shares they own give clues to changes in corporate power and control.

7. The proxy also lists the nominees for Board of Directors, with their age, number of shares owned, business background, and other corporate and major nonprofit affiliations. A thoughtful stockholder should wonder whom a nominee will represent. If the number of shares owned is

insignificant and the nominee obviously doesn't need the director's fees, why is he there? Surely not to battle for stockholders' rights. He's probably a member of the "good old boys' interlocking directors club." They serve on each other's boards, help raise money for each other's charities, and do business with each other as clients and suppliers. Together they preserve the status quo.

8. Compensation and options granted and special benefits must be disclosed, together with the potential value of the options, under assumed rates of appreciation of the stock at 5% and 10%, until the expiration date of the option. For example, some CEOs of major conglomerates realized tens of millions each in stock options in 1996 alone. Needless to say, they controlled their boards and had a lot of shares, once you add all the shares held by their relatives and trusts. Since the stockholders may also have done well that year, few probably complained or had the power to do anything about it. On the proxy statement benefits or "other compensation" are indicated by a dollar amount, which may include bonuses; insurance for home, auto, and life; use of the corporate plane, train car, and limo and driver; rent for second and third homes, etc. While this is a hypothetical future value, it gives you some idea of what the compensation really is.

9. The proxy must contain a graph that compares the cumulative total shareholder's return on the company's common stock over the last five years with the cumulative total return of the Standard & Poor's (S&P) 500 Stock Index or a peer group index of representative companies in the same industry, selected to reflect the general results of that industry over the same period. Your company may have had a good year, but if the S&P or the representative industry index was even better, you might wonder why your company lagged behind.

10. Proposals to increase authorized common stock or preferred stock are also in the proxy materials, as are proposed change in state of incorporation, change in the num-

ber of directors, shareholders' proposed motions (rarely favored by management and rarely able to pass), proposals to merge or divest of major divisions, selection of auditors, and so on. All of this affects you, the shareholder, and how your company will perform in the future.

A wise stockholder is a careful reader. Quarterly reports, annual reports, and proxy materials will give you plenty to read, and learn from.

CHAPTER ELEVEN

Chartists and Such

There are places in this world where you call in a witch doctor when you want to know the future. He kills a chicken, studies its entrails, then tells you about the future. The closest thing we have on Wall Street is the mighty and all-knowing "chartist." Chartists believe that, by studying what happened in the past, you can tell what will happen in the future.

A Wall Street chart is a graphic representation of the price and volume of trades of a stock over a period of time. The chartists insist that it's comparable to the X ray and brain scans a doctor studies to find what's going on in a human body. These charts are pictures designed to help the viewer understand the relationship of diverse facts and figures.

Charts are absolutely uncanny in pointing out signals of and clues to impending great movements in the past. But, alas, I've never known one to correctly foretell such action into the future. Occasionally, chartists do stick their necks out and make a firm prediction. If it doesn't happen the way they predicted, though, they go back and find some aberration in the chart that they missed. The chart was right, they claim, they just interpreted it incorrectly. They insist that what happened in the past will repeat in the future, and by going back far enough, they find examples of repetitive action and treat it as cause and effect.

Price and volume of shares traded reflects what has happened in the marketplace and what is going on in the world. There are thousands of reasons why a stock is sold and thousands more why a stock is bought. Decisions made in the future, not the patterns of the past, will determine the price of stocks. When the pattern is repeated, it's a coincidence.

The chartists huddle over their charts and study them like the gospel or the cryptic writings of Wall Street soothsayers. They use a special language and special symbols and hope that the way to untold riches will be revealed to the faithful. Signs like "Head and Shoulders," "Cup & Handle," "Double-Bottom Pine Patterns," and "High Tight Flag" are the "open sesame" of the chartists' world.

I believe that charts are an easy and effective way to see what happened in the past, but not necessarily a light into the future. Try to understand what's happening in the real world that will affect your stockholdings and your future and don't worry about charting.

There is also another group with strong views about how the market works. They are the devout followers of the "efficient market theory."

I must confess that it was only a few years ago that I first heard of the "efficient market theory." The occasion was a cocktail party arranged to introduce the wife of a younger friend and colleague. I was intrigued and much impressed; the wife had gone back to school on scholarship to get her MBA and was graduating cum laude. The conversation was definitely business-oriented.

At one point, I asked the young woman, "And how are you doing in the market?"

Her answer bowled me over. "Oh, I'd never go into the market. You can never find any bargains there!"

"What do you mean?" I asked, really curious now.

"Well," she continued, "in a free market, the price of

any stock is always maintained at exactly what it's worth. You see, it's all explained in 'the efficient market theory.' The price is a reflection of all the risks and rewards factored together, a balance of all the good or bad facts about the company and its future. And so you can see, there are no bargains. When the price goes down, it's because the risks are greater, and when the price goes up, the potential has increased. If you make any money, it's primarily luck."

"Haven't you ever known anyone who has made money in the market?"

"Of course, but it's just luck—dumb luck!"

The "efficient market," phooey! There's no such animal. This theory flies only in the halls of academe. All the facts and information about any given company in the market are never known. What information is available comes out in bits and pieces and is used by people with differing objectives. The market is not a computer. The bid and asked prices are set by people, and they are not computers either. The market is affected by emotions as well as reason. There are styles as well as trends. There is foresight and vision, courage and despair. Above all, there are hundreds of strategies that people bring to the game. The efficient market theory reminds me of the aeronautical engineer who proved that a bumblebee couldn't possibly fly!

CHAPTER TWELVE

Money Alert for Women

"Equal pay for equal work" was the battle cry. Women everywhere denounced the economic discrimination that resulted in their getting only 60% to 80% of the wages paid to men for the same work. Even today, the glass ceiling still keeps most women from getting to the top of the big salary and benefits pyramid. Since money so affects the quality of everyone's life, women's anger and frustration are understandable.

There is, however, a moneymaking opportunity for women that is almost completely free of discrimination. Wall Street is an equal opportunity area where men and women are usually treated the same. Hardly anyone cares whether a stockholder is a man or a woman. The rules and regulations of the SEC, the NYSE, NASD, and all other money markets are the same for everyone.

This being said, it is important to note that, until recently, the typical male broker was not very sensitive to the investment strategies and questions of many women investors. The good old boy network did not give the same tips to female clients, certainly not on the annual golf outings, and rarely at lunches hosted by the brokers. That is finally changing now that more women are working as brokers and women are making their own investment decisions and relying less on trust officers and other money mangers.

Because men on average die younger than women,

women have been controlling a lot more money. Many women brokers have become fabulously successful by being sensitive to some of the differences women investors bring to the Street. Women brokers are finally breaking through and serving their clients—female and male—very well. If you are a woman who finds herself assigned to a broker who treats you like a character in Ibsen's *A Doll's House,* report him to his boss and ask for another broker.

Like the laws of nature, the laws of the free market do not discriminate between the sexes. When you step off a cliff, you will fall like a rock whether you're a man or a woman. When there are more buyers than sellers, the price goes up; more sellers than buyers, the price goes down. The free market doesn't care a hoot whether a buyer or a seller is a man or a woman.

Well, you might say, isn't this true for any business activity in our free market economy? Women can be entrepreneurs, buy or sell real estate, run a corporation, manufacture products, or provide a service, and a thousand other enterprises. Ah yes, but in most cases, there is no anonymity. People you do business with know or can easily find out who owns the business. While there are many successful women entrepreneurs, there are also tales of women who could not overcome the hurdles of the good old boys' clubs while raising capital or getting loans.

But this need not be true in the stock market! No one has ever rejected delivery of a thousand shares of AT&T because it was owned by a woman or voided a trade because the buyer was not a man. That's why I find it sad that there are not more women making it on Wall Street. I'm not referring to employment. Thousands of women earn their living in the financial world, and many are extremely successful, despite the hurdles. They are registered reps, analysts, portfolio managers, market makers, mutual fund and annuity salespeople, and even partners in some of the firms. I wonder why the majority of women aren't playing the market for their own account. Where are the women who manage their own money for income and growth, women who achieve a higher standard of living for themselves and their families by increasing their capital through Wall Street? The small number of women who are active in the market is particularly perplexing, since women control the greater part of the wealth in this country. Perhaps because a large part of the wealth women control was acquired through inheritance or widowhood, they may feel compelled to preserve it and pass it on, through trust officers or money managers, rather than to risk increasing it themselves.

Some women may feel they do not have the proper training and education to compete in the market. Nonsense! Most men don't know what they're doing when they get started either. Lack of exposure and experience is easily overcome by both men and women who choose to learn. The millions of intelligent, disciplined, and ambitious women who do make it in the market find it easier than they thought it would be when they started.

The initial capital to play the market comes to women the same way it comes to me: through work, sacrifice, and savings. IRA rollovers, pension plans, and outplacement severance following a downsizing have served as a wonderful starter for many women and men to enter the market. The chance to manage your own retirement funds is a wonderful and relatively easy way to start with low-risk investments. You can learn the basics about stocks and bonds through books and classes and the financial press, but the real learning experience comes with doing. The sooner you start, the richer you'll be.

In the stock market, when you manage your own money, thee is no need for anyone else to give you a break; you make your own opportunities, and your success is determined by how well you perceive things as they really are and how quickly you recognize clues that foreshadow what will work in the future. This calls for hard work, close attention to the relevant numbers and facts, and, finally, the courage to act on what you believe.

Intuition is a wonderful gift here. If you think you smell something fishy, you probably do. Women usually do not take wild fliers with the family's security—that kind of caution will make you a real star on Wall Street.

There's no guarantee that your decisions will always be right, but at least you have the comfort of knowing you're not playing with a deck stacked against your sex. Wall Street is an equal opportunity arena, with enough hazards and rewards for everyone. Jump in!

CHAPTER THIRTEEN

The Cutting Edge

Wall Street can be a school of hard knocks. And there are some who have been wiped out financially who remember it as a great finishing school. But Wall Street can also be the ultimate graduate school for the ever-evolving boundaries of science and industry. True, it is a self-actualizing school. There are no formal classes and no teachers, but there are wonderful "textbooks," which describe and explain the new science or technology. These textbooks are known as IPO (initial public offering) prospectuses.

The potential for commercial application of a scientific discovery creates a need for capital. The prospect of a new way to make money is almost irresistible to entrepreneurs when there is a scientific breakthrough. Like mushrooms that sprout up overnight, new IPO's flood the Street, inviting investors to exploit the new science. The prospectus describes the new science or discovery and explains, in terms even laypeople can understand, what it means, how it works, and how it will be applied or used.

As a result, there has been a fantastic expansion in the scientific knowledge available to the public. Never in our history has the cutting edge of science been so available to and understood by laypeople. Knowledge is every expanding, but in the past, new discoveries were attractive only to the scientists, academics, and intellectuals. In today's free market society, there is a powerful incentive to be informed.

The investing public can profit from new technology and applied science; this is a gold mine for venture capitalists.

Reading prospectuses of IPOs can be more than an opportunity to make money, it can also be a wonderful way of continuing your education. How else would you have learned about new discoveries first presented by investment bankers or venture capitalists?

They include: monoclonal antibodies for diagnostics and therapeutics; applications of microchips to medicine; biodegradable hydrophilic polymers for drug delivery; oral delivery and transmucosal drug delivery systems; plant derived high value-added products such as plastics, fat substitutes, inks, etc.; composite materials for industry; artificial organs; subreceptor targeted drugs; computer technologies such as networking; cellular phone technology; bioremediation processes; carbohydrate drugs; artificial blood; advanced imaging technologies; interactive telecommunications; and artificial skin.

The list is staggering.

In these "frontiers of science" ventures, it is the sizzle rather than the steak that raises the capital. The glamour and the promise of tomorrow often raise the demand for stock and prices go to delirious levels. Ironically, this can go on for years, despite little commercial success of the company.

But there often comes a time when the investor says, "No more waiting. This could take forever. I think I'll look for something else." When enough stockholders feel this way, the price collapses and the company must deliver more than sizzle to get back on track.

Fortunately, this happens often enough to create new investors for venture capital. Think of the revolutionary changes that have ocurred during your own lifetime, because of new techniques, new companies, new ventures.

CHAPTER FOURTEEN

The Challenge

Some years ago I had lunch with the late Peter Grace, one of the most famous entrepreneurs of his time. It was at the Princeton Club on the hottest day of the decade. Although I had only three blocks to walk, I was completely drenched with perspiration when I got there. My host, then in his late sixties, was limp as well because he had made a one-hour trip from Long Island. After finishing our lunch and business, we drifted into a philosophical discussion of life and the pressure we all faced. A question I had long wanted to ask broke out: "You are obviously very successful, with probably more money then you could ever need, yet here you are making an exhausting physical effort in pursuit of another business deal when you could retire and luxuriate in your golden years."

His answer provided me with an insight into what makes us tick: "You know, we all enjoy, even relish, doing what we do well—I'm good at recognizing opportunities—building businesses, making things happen, making $2 + 2 = 7$. It gives me more pleasure than anything else I do. Why should I retire and hit some damn golf ball around just because everyone else does?"

How true. We tend to concentrate on what we do well, ever trying to do even better. Creating a better mousetrap brings us satisfaction and a genuine sense of self-worth. The savvy investor is always trying to do better; success spurs him on. The Wall Street game is fascinating and a challenge, even though making money may no longer be the prime consideration. What should you do when you know you've got enough to be comfortable for the rest of your life? Drop out of the game? Ridiculous!

Every game, whether it's chess or bridge or Monopoly, offers rewards. The challenge, the puzzle, and the search for the elusive solution create a world that is immeasurably satisfying. The Wall Street game presents an even greater challenge, because the rules constantly change.

Here's a case in point. Some years ago I bought a new issue, which became a typical example of the ups and downs, starts and stops, twists and turns that face every new company. I still don't know how this story will end, but it sure has my attention. This was a fairly new company pioneering the manufacture of diamond semiconductors, memory chips, and blue lasers. Management was high-tech engineers who split from a large computer corporation to start their own business. Although they hadn't made any profits after two years, they were close to break even— primarily because of government research contracts to develop new technologies. They had many patents, and the money raised was to be used for developing applications for the new technologies.

The initial offering price was to be at $9. In light of the great potential, it seemed reasonable to me, despite the company's negative P/E ratio and the low book value. I indicated an interest in some shares. My broker laughed, "You'll be lucky if I can get you any at all."

A few weeks later he called to say that the new issue market had cooled somewhat and the price had dropped to $7. "Did you still want the shares?" Even with the stock price 25% lower, there was less interest in the stock, but the number of shares to be offered had also been reduced by 12%. The IPO was finally completed, and I took the shares because I thought it was an even better deal than before. Trading started and it hovered around the offering price for months.

The first quarterly statement indicated more of the same. The price began to drop as the holders who had bought for a quick new issue profit got discouraged and sold. It finally hit \$5. Since nothing else had changed, I bought more shares at $5^1/_2$. Sales went from \$7 million in 1992 to \$10 million in 1993 and \$15 million in 1995, with little better than breakeven in profit. Additional contracts with the government and prominent semiconductor companies to develop new technologies reinforced the belief that this company knew what it was doing. The price moved up in 1995, and there was a secondary offering for a million shares at $12^1/_2$.

This created more interest in and awareness of the company, and the price reached a high of 17 in 1996. I visited the plant with a friend who was a specialist in electronic engineering, and we were both impressed by the plant, the employees, and the efficiency of the operation. The company had already been granted fifty patents and seventy more were pending.

I bought more shares at 14 and within a month it dropped to 11 bid, $11^1/_4$ offered. What's wrong? I wondered. Is anything wrong? Do I buy more or do I wait for the dust to settle? In 1996 the stock was $12^1/_2$. I held, of course. By June of 1997 the price hit $29^1/_2$. I wondered whether to sell now and go smiling to the bank or whether I should follow my own advice. I'm still holding on to the stock.

So it is with Wall Street—the most fascinating game of all. Stimulating, challenging, prodding you to stay on your toes, constantly attacking and expanding the boundaries— like the tales of Scheherazade, never ending.

Part Two

Strategies for Successful Investing

A few years ago I went through the sobering process of making my will and adjusting my financial affairs. The pros and cons of each decision touched off great frustration. What was I leaving them? Tangible things, yes, but what I'd really like to leave my dear ones is what I've learned. Property is tangible and sterile, subject to depreciation, loss, or simply consumption. The precious things are what I've learned in my journey through life: how to create, build, and preserve; what people are about and why.

Out of this necessarily reflective process came the Oakwood Harbour Investment Seminars, with an extremely selective and intelligent student body—my family. We met every Saturday afternoon during one whole summer, and I talked with them about the market and the world of business, answered questions, and, more important, asked them questions.

There was plenty of homework. Each student was required to spend two hours of research and study for every hour spent in class. The textbooks were current prospectuses, that is, IPOs and secondary offerings. We went over them page by page and explored the significance of each paragraph. We studied the financials, broke out each line of the balance sheet and income statement, discussed what it represented and how it fit into the whole picture. In time, my family came to appreciate this aspect of our seminars because it gave them some idea of what a corporation was worth in dollars.

Then they learned how to examine a business itself, its competitive position, the size of the market, and its potential. We discussed the officers and their management expertise, the investors, their backgrounds, and the interest each had in the business in terms of equity, salary, or options.

Next, they learned to appraise the price per share paid by insiders, the price to the public, the effect of the dilution and risks on the company's future. Every bit of the prospectus was examined and assessed. Our examination of corporate thinking provided the class with information each member would use before making a decision about buying the stock.

Interestingly, at the beginning, the women were much better at all of this than the men. They were more suspicious; they questioned much that the men accepted. As many more prospectuses were studied, the men caught up and became more skeptical of the printed word, too, and better judgments were made by all.

By the end of the summer I had the comforting feeling that I no longer had to worry. They had learned to use the magic word "why" as a key to unlocking the parts before making a decision. For their final assignment, they had to select a stock they would recommend to the group and buy it with their own money. They did me proud. I bought some stock in each company they suggested and was successful on all except one. It had the sweetest rise of all—at one time it traded at eight times what I paid, but since I didn't buy much and it was a small OTC company, I rarely followed it. I ended up with nothing after it finally went broke. Sometimes I don't pay enough attention; lots of lessons for me in the seminar, too!

Here's a quick summary list of ideas—bequests—I hope will help you find financial security:

- Never sell unless you have a compelling reason. Sending your broker's kids to college is not a compelling reason!
- Run your own money. Nobody is as interested in it as you.
- Choose your securities as you choose your clothes. They should fit *you*.
- What's appropriate for your most successful friend may be all wrong for you.
- The magic word for understanding investments is "why." Keep asking "why" until you understand.
- Nibble and savor before you take a big bite.
- Inside information clouds your judgment.
- Anticipation is the wind beneath the wings of price.
- The jury is out until you actually sell.
- The great scores are made by perceiving reality better than the marketplace does.
- The realization that the emperor has no clothes can make you rich.

CHAPTER FIFTEEN

Strategy One—Over the Counter Leads to Success

The strategy most widely used by quiet millionaires is to look for opportunities that are less competitive. You have a better chance to get results when you're not battling thousands of investors just as smart as you are and trying to gather the same harvest. Robert Frost once advised, "I took the [road] less traveled by / And that has made all the difference."

As applied to Wall Street, the road less traveled is the over-the-counter (OTC) market. It is estimated that there are over 50,000 public companies in the United States. About 3,000 are traded on the New York Stock Exchange (NYSE) and 2,000 on the American Stock Exchange (ASE). There are perhaps another five hundred on all the regional exchanges. That means approximately 44,500 companies are traded OTC—"over the counter." What of it?

Well, the listed companies are usually the largest and most important, with widely held securities. Therefore, they reflect the greatest public investment. This results in attracting the greatest attention. Their activity is reported minute by minute via the stock tape and computer. Newspapers, television, radio, magazines, and newsletters provide a fishbowl atmosphere in which every corporate twitch is immediately interpreted and some action contemplated. The overwhelming bulk of managed money (i.e., pension plans, mutual funds, trusts, and corporate investments) is invested in these listed securities.

The OTC market is actually the most important market for the investor who wants to become a quiet millionaire. While it does contain some large and widely known companies, as MCI Communications, Apple Computer, Grey Advertising, Microsoft, and Security Bankcorp, it is made up primarily of small, less popular public companies whose stockholders number in the low thousands or even hundreds. The small corporate size and smaller stockholders base account for the lack of interest and attention that most OTC companies get. They are not written up or analyzed on a regular basis. Before the NASDAQ Composite Index, it was hard even to get quotes for many of them on a daily basis.

There are still thousands of the smaller public companies that are not listed on the NASDAQ Composite Index. This makes it much harder to study and follow them; however, it also ensures far less competition for the investment opportunities they present.

By and large, the OTC market is the breeding ground for newly hatched public companies. These infant companies, like infants everywhere, have the greatest potential for growth and also, alas, for early demise. It is in this market that you will find opportunities to invest in the cutting edge of science—like the new companies trying to find a commercial use for genetic engineering, space exploration, medical technology, and the communication superhighway. Also among these companies are new adventures in marketing, distribution, finance, for example.

There is also little frenetic competition while you are deciding what to do. Every company publishes an annual report and many even furnish quarterly statements. The larger ones must file annual and quarterly reports with the SEC. These are obtainable from the companies or the SEC for a small fee. The reports contain information required by the commission and the law. They may provide the potential investor with the facts he or she needs to make a decision.

In the final analysis the market is people: what they think about the future; who's got the ball; who wants the ball, and what will they do with it? In the OTC companies, you are dealing with human beings, not inanimate institutions. The president of a small public company is probably the largest single stockholder; he is usually also the founder and prime mover. It's possible to meet him and talk to him at the annual meeting or by phone or appointment. You can make a judgment about him. Do you trust him? Is he a winner, loser, or phony? Do you want to put a bet on his performance and future? This is almost impossible with a listed company. You're a stockholder; so what?! There are tens of thousands of stockholders. Do you think the president has nothing better to do than meet with you or answer your questions?

In the OTC market, it's possible to acquire a significant number of shares of a company with a relatively small investment. Many of the companies are capitalized below $10 million, and there are some below $1 million. The Street term for them is small cap companies. Often, lack of interest or poor visibility results in their common stock's trading below book value. Thus it's possible for the independent investor to accumulate a significant percentage of the company (i.e., from 1 to 10%).

There are requirements that you file with the SEC when you own 5% or more. Five % of peanuts is still peanuts! Ah yes, but the tiny fingers and hands of an infant grow with the baby, and when the baby grows, every part grows proportionately. When that infant company reaches maturity, your 5% may represent a very impressive amount.

A word of warning: Perennial scandals involving OTC scams should make every securities investor wary of the unknown cold-call broker who offers a little-known stock as a sure thing, a way to get rich quick.

A favorite ploy is to recommend a stock at a fairly low price and not push too hard for a sale. Then a short time later, he'll call you again and tell you how well the stock has done and how sorry he is that you missed it. Of course he is nice enough to have another "winner" for you!

Quiet millionaires don't fall for these scams and don't expect to get rich quickly. Intelligent research, knowing and trusting your broker, and finding legitimate companies will prevent you from being taken by unscrupulous wheeler-dealers.

CHAPTER SIXTEEN

Strategy Two—Follow the Winners

There's one quiet millionaire who always makes me feel good when I think of her. She was widowed in her mid-thirties and left with four young children. Her husband had been a veteran and a civil service employee, so there were some death benefits. She converted their rambling one-family house in Brooklyn into a boardinghouse. The low rent and the opportunity for renters to become boarders with meals made her place attractive and popular.

Hattie was always friendly and cheerful. She welcomed help with the kids, and the emotionally starved boarders were delighted to pitch in. Everyone felt important. She was constantly asking for advice with her problems—one human trusting another.

The boardinghouse flourished, and in a few years she expanded and bought another house alongside her own. Her emphasis shifted and she became more of a landlady. With the children in school and fewer meals to prepare, she had more time. She went with real estate brokers to look for houses she could buy for no cash down, then fix them up for rooming. Hard work, but she had her share of good buys and successes.

Then one very hot day, the real estate broker said,

"Let's stop off here and cool off a bit." It was a Bache stock-broker's office and fully air conditioned. The huge room was divided into two parts. A large lounge area with chairs and tables covered with stock literature was arranged so cus-tomers and potential customers could watch the overhead tape, which reflected the action on the NYSE and the ASE. The rest of the room contained the stockbrokers' desks and telephones. Clerks were running around with pieces of paper and important things to do.

It was all very exciting and wonderfully refreshing to Hattie. Soon she was talking to the customers seated around her. Most of them were retired men who spent their days at the broker's, keeping an eye on their investments and shar-ing the business gossip of the moment. (This was many years before you could do this on your personal computer or cable TV channel at home, as is the case today.) Many had been very successful in business and were now making money in the market. Hattie's naïveté about the market was apparent to all, and her loud, cheerful voice reached every corner of the room. Despite the laughter at her expense, she took it all good-naturedly and kept asking questions.

Hattie had discovered the market. She became a regu-lar at the Bache office, and it was a rare day indeed that she didn't turn up for a least half a day. Within a few years, Hat-tie was on her way to becoming a quiet millionaire.

You may be wondering about Hattie's special invest-ment strategy. Actually, it was rooted in her survival tech-nique. She was not afraid to ask for help—she did it successfully as a young widow with four kids. She sought, accepted, and appreciated help wherever she could find it. This was her genius. She made friends easily and could read people. She knew almost instantly whom she could trust and whom to stay away from. Among the twenty to thirty "regu-lars" at the Bache office, there was a great range in market savvy. Some were consistent winners, others invariable losers. Hattie never became a very sophisticated investor, but she could pick the customers who were, and she would follow their advice. She was adept at getting information and sharing it. Many of the smartest customers did not talk to one another because of jealousy or some past slight, but Hattie talked to everyone, so she always had the advantage of everyone's advice.

Hattie's fortune has grown and so have her children— all college graduates, all married with good jobs—but alas none with Hattie's gift for friendship and ability to follow winners.

CHAPTER SEVENTEEN

Strategy Three—Legal Insider Trading

Let me tell you the story of Jane, who is a quiet millionaire and uses another popular strategy I call "legal insider trading." Perhaps she hasn't fulfilled all of her financial goals just yet, but she's still a young woman, and rounding out a million dollars or two for her is really only a question of time. Her strategy for making it in the market reflects her background and station in life. At age thirty-five she was an assistant professor of history without tenure at a prestigious university. Although she was aware of the market in a rather casual way because some of her wedding gifts had been securities, she had never really explored it.

Then she was denied tenure. In desperation she looked around for some other way to make a living. Wall Street presented a possible solution. She read everything she could find about the stock market in the university library. What might have been overwhelming for most of us was catnip to her. She went through book after book, absorbed theory after theory, and in a short time, she began to buy and sell along the guidelines of the last theory she had read. But, unfortunately, the neat techniques that worked so well in the last book did not work the same when she applied them in the real world.

But the professor was a scholar, and a good one; she persisted in her studies and finally found a method she liked, and that worked for her. Instead of following the latest tip sheets, broker's recommendations, or analyst's reports, she became a student of "insider trading."

The SEC's definition of an insider—an officer, director, or owner of 5% or more of the company's stock—is specific because it is designed to give early notice to the public that management, in a position to have special knowledge, has taken some action vis-à-vis the stock. The SEC requires an insider to file a report with the commission whenever he or she buys or sells any company security. These reports are open to the public. There are services that monitor both listed and unlisted public companies and report such insider trades to their subscribers.

Jane's university library was a subscriber to such a service, and she found it fascinating reading. She pored over the reports for the previous two or three years and applied the magic word "why?" to any of the trades or pattern of trades that seemed unusual.

In a relatively short time, she realized that insider trading was significant when stock was bought rather than sold. An insider might sell some stock because he had some foreshadowing of bad news for the company, but if that were so, he would try to sell as much as he could. That would drive down the price of the stock and also draw a lot of attention from the analysts and traders. Most of the time, she discovered, insiders sell for other reasons. They need cash to see their kids through college or to buy another home, a larger boat, sometimes, just to remove some of the eggs from that heavy corporate basket. Insider selling, she learned, may be important, but most of the time, it's not. (The temptation for insiders to sell short is another ball game altogether. More on this very risky strategy in chapter 21.)

Insider buying is a different story. Why do insiders buy?

Because the stock represents greater value than the current price. That "greater value" may be defined as greater leverage for control of the company, or as something good that is going to happen to the company, or as growth and performance that will probably result in higher price for the stock in some future market.

The professor decided that she could share in this "greater value." Her research revealed that many of the companies had indeed done remarkably well within a year or two of insider buying.

She also checked to see whether there had been any recent adverse developments. Disaster can destroy the best-laid plans of a company. Jane began to nibble at some companies and to monitor their price, performance, and, of course, insider trading. When insiders bought more, Jane bought more. She used several brokers and was amused when each of them, one way or another, said, "Where do you get these odd 'cats and dogs'?"

She was patient and prudent and her strategy has paid off handsomely. She's been in the market for four years now, and her initial capital has increased eightfold. Her biggest problem—and the biggest problem with this strategy—is knowing when to sell. She knows when and what to buy but finds it very hard to know when to sell. The insiders probably have different goals from hers and different restraints. For the time being, she sells when there has been a very big move, anywhere from 100% to 1000% over her initial investment, and there is also an opportunity to invest money in another company she has uncovered and tracked.

As Jane became more sophisticated about Wall Street, she expanded her insider trading group to include people and institutions that knew more about the company and the working world of Wall Street than she did, people who were movers and shakers, who had a reputation for making things happen.

When such people began to accumulate the stock of a public company, they weren't necessarily required to file with the SEC as they were not officers, directors, or owners of 5%. Newspapers and financial publications, though, constantly report stock acquisition by high-profile people in companies other that the ones they control. It's a kind of Wall Street gossip that provides smoke that may hide fire. Jane followed these kinds of stories closely.

Jane also realized that there were other "insiders" who could provide important clues: almost any employee of a company she was watching. If someone you know buys stock in a company he works for and the answer you get when you ask why is "We're doing great. We have some new products that are going to sweep the market," you can usually take their advice to the bank.

Sometimes you have an "insider" who doesn't even work for the company and isn't an officer or director. An old school chum of mine, who became a laundry man, told me one day he wanted to buy five hundred shares of Acme Radio Co. He had never been in the market before, and so I asked why? His answer was classic "street smarts": "I'm their towel man. For two years I've delivered towels every week. They started with 12 towels a week and by the end of the year it was 40 towels a week. In the last three months they've gone from 120 to 200. You don't have to be a genius to know something is going on, so I'd like a piece of it." He was so right—special "insider" knowledge.

Another early clue legal inside traders like to follow with interest is news that the XYZ fund, for example, controlled by a Wall Street innovator and leader, was buying stock. There are relatively easy ways to learn which funds or institutions own stock in a public company: Standard & Poor's reports, Value Line reports, etc. In addition, the annual statements of the company you're interested in records a list of important stockholders, quantity and percentage owned.

This kind of knowledge is not an "open sesame" to a fortune; it's only a clue. Even the gurus make mistakes and, quite often, the actions they recommend will not work to achieve your goal. The mutual funds, for example, may be buying a particular company or industry to arrive at a pre-arranged balance in their holdings for very long-term goals or for defensive reasons, such as to protect the fund if the market has a shakeout. A particular stock may not drop as much during a shakeout. Or the fund manager may have promised to buy the stock simply to thank someone for a block of stock he received in a good new issue.

The same kinds of reasons may account for the personal holdings of a security analyst or fund manager. The very fact you were able to get the information that they own a stock may be no accident. They may be promoting the stock and thus reveal their position in order to induce you to buy it. And, of course, there must be times when a president or the major stockholder buys more stock in his own company to show that he has confidence that the stock will go higher—or maybe he is planning big changes in the company and hopes that you will be encouraged to buy and to help him drive the price up. There's a whole school of followers who track insider activity and trade accordingly. It's a clue, but you should find better evidence before you make your move.

When an insider sells, it doesn't necessarily mean the company is in trouble. His corporate stock may represent the bulk of his net worth, and his accountant may have told him it's important to begin estate planning and to diversify. Even when he protests, "The stock will go higher; my company is growing," a good financial advisor may respond, "Good, the stock you still have will be worth more, but at the same time we won't have all your eggs in one basket if anything should go wrong." It's important to remember that a management insider may be selling for any number of reasons other than bad news about the business. He may need cash to pay taxes, to buy another business, to finance a divorce, or to buy a vacation home.

As Jane found out, it is usually more significant when insiders buy, particularly, when several insiders buy. They are certainly more privy to what's going on and in a position to see farther into the future of the company than you are. It's a clue and an invitation to do further checking.

Another kind of insider buying that calls for attention is when the corporation announces it is going to buy back a specific amount or percentage of its shares. It's not unreasonable to conclude that the corporation thinks its stock is underpriced and that it is buying a bargain. This usually occurs when the company is in a strong cash position or when the cost of money is cheap and the company has no immediate plans for acquisition or expansion. It can also mean a hostile takeover threat may be hovering and the company is "circling the wagons." The announcement of a buyback usually stiffens the price of the stock, so many individual traders rush to buy it in anticipation that the corporation will have to pay more to acquire the amount of stock it wants.

Historically, only 40% of announced buybacks actually occur. In 1995 1,108 public companies announced buybacks for a collective value of $98.9 billion. It is believed that about $40 billion was actually bought back; the balance of the stock in play either rose so high that it did not warrant the buyback, or the buyback was announced to move the stock up. There are dozens of cases when the stock is, in fact, bought back by the company, but the stock nevertheless drifts lower. Remember, an announced buyback is only a clue; you still need more information.

There is a theory that buybacks, mergers, acquisitions, and public companies going private reduce the number of shares and securities available on Wall Street and thus shrink the market. With fewer shares and ever more buyers with money, the price must go up. I disagree. New stocks are constantly available through secondary issues and initial public offerings, stock splits or dividends. And the money is not lockstepped to Wall Street. There's a constant shifting of financial interests, for example, in real estate, joint ventures, and overseas investments. The basic good sense of investors stops them from paying too much for a stock. At a certain point, an investor says, "Hey, that price is beyond reason. I don't care who else is buying it; I'd rather invest in something else."

CHAPTER EIGHTEEN

Strategy Four—Follow Troubled Companies

Sam is a former NYSE broker, but today he shuns the responsibility of shepherding other people's capital and enjoys the luxury of running his own money. He accumulated enough to concentrate on working his particular specialty, bankruptcies. A reorganization to him is like the motherlode to a prospector. He told me this tale:

On a cloudy day not too many winters ago, an elderly minister clutched his overcoat against the wind as he left his church near the river. He noticed a haggard man standing on a bridge and staring intently at the dark water below. With a sense of foreboding, he hurried to the man's side and laid a friendly hand on his shoulder. The man reacted with a low moan as he came out of his trance.

"Can I help you, my son?" the minister asked gently.

A hollow laugh accompanied the response: "It's too late now—it's all over, but thanks anyway."

The minister's arm went around the man's shoulders and drew him close as he said, "Come along with me. Have a cup of hot tea and tell me all about it."

A short time later they were seated in the minister's study, their teacups already drained twice as the forlorn man sobbed out his story.

"I was a very successful businessman—had over a hundred employees—built it all from scratch. My parents were poor and I finished college at night, worked pretty hard, saved every penny. Then I started my own business. It grew and grew. I got married and had two wonderful children. I thought I was king of the world. Then somehow the business began to sour. I fell behind in some of my bills, so I borrowed to pay the Peters and Pauls who dunned me for money. Everything got worse. I had to pull my kids out of private schools. They repossessed my Cadillac and I had to let most of my employees go. I started to drink and my wife said she'd leave me. So, to tell you the truth, I was thinking of my insurance policy as I stared at the river—maybe my family will have something."

"Now, now," the minister interrupted, "things are never as bad as they seem. Cheer up. You must have faith. Here is a wonderful book, the bible. Take it, read it, you will find salvation there."

Refreshed and warmed, the weary man thanked him and left.

About a year and a half later the minister was startled to see a chauffer-driven limousine pull up outside his church. He responded to the doorbell and was astounded to see the man from the bridge. He was the picture of good health and cheer, dressed in an Armani suit and sporting a Rolex.

"I've come to express my gratitude and to make a contribution to your Minister's Fund. You saved me and my family from ruin."

Totally confused, the old minister asked, "How? What happened?"

"Well, it was that book you gave me. I'm not much of a believer, but when I got to my room I tossed it on the bed as I got undressed. The book had popped open, and then, just as you said, it was my salvation! As I started to read, in bold letters at the top of the page, it said, 'Chapter Eleven.' "

Chapter 11 is a special section of the bankruptcy law that in effect gives a debtor a chance to wipe the slate clean and start over. In the dark old days, if you owed money, you had to pay up or go to prison. Ironically, the debt continued to grow as interest was added until paid. Families struggling to survive with the breadwinner in jail did not make for a tranquil and prosperous society. The only salvation was to find someone who would pay the debt for them. Sometimes people had to become indentured servants to whoever would pay the debt just to avoid jail. Eventually bankruptcy laws were passed. A debtor now can declare bankruptcy and put all his assets up for distribution to the creditors. He is then freed from all past debts or obligations. The laws now also include corporations and even public companies.

When a public company becomes insolvent it may choose to take advantage of Chapter 11 of the U.S. bankruptcy law, which in effect gives the debtor (i.e., corporate management) a chance to continue to run the company while it tries to work out a settlement with its creditors, unions, landlords, etc., and to arrange for financing so the business does not have to be liquidated. This opportunity to reorganize is obtained by petition to the bankruptcy court and granted when the court thinks there is a reasonable chance that the debtor can carry it off.

Once the petition is issued, the list of creditors and litigants is frozen. The debtor stops all payments except for current service and supplies—and to the IRS, of course! Payment to any past creditor is deemed a preference and therefore a no no! This is a wonderful opportunity to straighten things out. Creditor committees are formed to determine what the company's assets are and to protect the respective interests of creditors and the company. Periodic reports must be made to the court and to demonstrate that the company's assets are not being wasted and that some progress is being made in negotiation with the various creditor committees.

All this takes time. Depending on the size and condition of the bankrupt company, working out a settlement can take several months to several years. The debtor tries to come up with a plan that the court will approve and that will be acceptable to a majority of the creditors. If, for example, the total owed is $180 million, those owed at least $90 million must vote for the plan. If the total number of creditors is 2,830, at least 1,416 must vote for it.

The plan usually provides for the creditors to get something less than the amount owed them. They are willing to take less in order to get something now—the bird-in-the-hand theory. Often what they get, in addition to or in lieu of cash, is some kind of security; equity stock, notes, preferred stock, bonds. Sometimes control of the company is transferred to new management to bring in fresh capital, which makes the settlement and reorganization possible.

During all the time the negotiations and maneuvering are going on, the securities of the public company in Chapter 11 are still being traded, and the prices fluctuate with the news and progress reported. Corporate operations are highly visible because of the court's supervision. Not every plan submitted to the court is accepted. There are all kinds of hearings, notices, reviews, etc. The judge tries to encourage a plan that will be fair to all the creditors, secured and unsecured, the bondholders, the preferred stockholders, and even the common stockholders (who are the last to be considered in a bankruptcy).

The final plan to be voted on by the creditors is well publicized, usually for several months before the vote. It is during this time that my friend Sam makes important investment moves. The whole bankruptcy procedure dredges up more information about the company, its plans and potential than even a prospectus gives you.

The market being what it is—usually overbought or oversold—you may have a great investment opportunity. Bankrupt stocks and bonds are usually oversold. Most money managers, analysts, and investors avoid bankrupt companies. They try to get them out of their portfolios because they don't want to be reminded of their mistakes. They think these companies are losers—too complicated, too unpredictable, they take too long to recover—you get the picture.

But companies coming out of Chapter 11 have some great advantages. There are no hidden liabilities, because the court invites everyone who has a claim or lien of any kind to come forward and get their share before the company is discharged from its Chapter 11 status. If they fail to do so, they are forever barred from making the claim. All onerous contracts with suppliers, distributors, unions, and landlords, are canceled, and the discharged company goes forth as unencumbered as a newborn babe. In addition, there is now adequate capital to ensure successful operation and a carry-forward tax loss to protect the first years of profit. By the time this all happens, the common stock is greatly diluted and the preferred stock and bonds changed or converted into something else.

Sam has made several substantial moves by following and investing in reorganizations, because there is a time lag between the creation of the opportunity and the true assessment or evaluation of what the security is worth.

Public company reorganizations are so complex and take such a long time that very few brokers or investors follow them. They do not offer the kinds of investment opportunities that registered reps or money managers like. The typical broker likes to recommend stock that can be watched from day to day, that will offer a chance for a quick profit and, of course, a quick commission. He also likes to make recommendations that can be defended because everyone else is recommending the same stock. Typical brokers feel so strongly about this that occasionally a broker's confirmation slip will note, "This security has been unsolicited by the broker"—i.e., not recommended here!

A classic example of the excitement and opportunity that a reorganization can offer is the history of the Chicago Milwaukee Corporation, a conglomerate whose prime asset was a bankrupt railroad. Chicago Milwaukee was forced to seek the protection of the bankruptcy court in late 1977 because its disappearing cash flow had made it insolvent. The dumping of its stock drove the price down to $3 per share in 1978. Over the next three years, there was a wonderful opportunity to accumulate the stock at bargain prices; although the stock hit a high of $20 in April 1980, it dropped back to $10 in the fall. Few of the stockholders or financial experts realized that it was a steal even at $20.

The Chicago Milwaukee had everything: a large carryforward tax loss, tremendous unrecognized assets (the bankrupt railroad was carried on the books as a pittance), and an unappreciated subsidiary, the Milwaukee Land Company, with huge landholdings. As various parts of the corporation were sold, the prices realized dramatized the potential for the assets it still retained. The price of the stock continued to rise. In 1981 it flirted with the $80s; in 1983 it broke $110; and in mid-1984 the common stock exceeded $150.

If you were one of those quiet investors who followed your own mind and bought 1,000 shares in 1978 at $3 a share, for a total investment of $3,000, and if you held on—despite all the opportunities to cash in big—until the summer of 1984, your $3,000 worth of stock was worth $150,000.

There is another more recent example with which you may be familiar. Federated Department Stores was at one time the largest operator of department stores in the United States, with more than 550 stores in thirty-six states, including some of the most famous and venerable names in the industry, such as Bloomingdale's, Rich's, Stern's, and the Broadway chain in the Midwest. Nevertheless, it foundered and was forced into bankruptcy. After much negotiating and pushing and pulling, a plan was developed and finally approved by creditors and bankers, to take them out of bankruptcy.

Federated flowered after emerging from bankruptcy on February 10, 1992. Stock on that day traded at $15^1/_2$. Its cleaned up financial picture, carry-forward tax loss, and pared down overhead enabled the company to make a series of aggressive department store acquisitions. By 1998 the stock traded as high as 50, and the consensus of Wall Street analysts was that it would go even higher.

So you don't have to go back to ancient times to find opportunities. Investing in Federated in 1992 didn't involve too complicated a picture—no high-tech language to figure out, no scientific jargon to interpret—just an ordinary retail operation given a second chance. And a way to triple your investment in five years!

CHAPTER NINETEEN

Strategy Five—Small Cap Companies

Ben is a product of New York. He was born on the Lower East Side of Manhattan, when the melting pot of New York City was primarily in its chicken soup phase. His parents were very poor and, as the oldest of four children, he hit the streets early. The tough dollars he earned helped keep the family alive and together. He graduated from errand boy to newspaper route to ice cream vendor, but there is some question as to whether he graduated from high school. No matter. He worked hard, expanded his ice cream operation, and by the time he was drafted in World War II, he was making a good enough living.

The army experience was a revelation and an education. He made friends everywhere and was amazed to see how well off all his army buddies were compared with him. Among his bunk mates was a stockbroker who was rich and seemed to make money from doing nothing. Strangely enough, he continued to make money while he was in basic training and even after they were shipped overseas. Even stranger, the broker was a lousy poker player and not nearly as smart as some of the other guys.

All of this made an impression on Ben, and he was determined to find out more about the stock market if he got out of the army alive. He did. With his poker money, savings, and bonus, Ben got married and went into the hot dog pushcart business. He did well, developed his regular spots, and built a following of steady customers who liked his cheerful, friendly, personal touch.

But there were times in the long day when Ben had a chance to read the papers while he waited for the next customer. He developed a taste for the financial pages. Eventually, he was intrigued enough to drop into a brokerage office near his hot dog post. In a short time, he began to play the market. Fortunately, the market was in an upswing and almost everything he tried did well. This encouraged him, and he became more active. But eventually the pendulum began to swing back, and Ben slowly but definitely began to give back the profit he had made. He also began to realize that his broker was not such a genius—because he lost some of his own money, too. A very sobering experience!

There was one silver cloud in this dark sky. The broker made commissions whether the market went up or down. Surely this was better than selling hot dogs. Becoming a registered representative became Ben's goal and passion. He studied, did the homework, and eventually passed the test and became a broker. He even got a job with the same firm with which he had made his first trades. The years of hustling on the streets stood him in good stead. He made friends easily, sized up situations quickly, and acted decisively. His clients and followers grew, and soon he was making more money than he had ever dreamed possible.

As he became more sophisticated, however, he began to seek out opportunities that appealed to him rather than those recommended by his firm. He was reprimanded and told to stick to listed stocks, more particularly, to those that were followed and analyzed by the firm's experts. But Ben's experience was that he and his customers did better with the "cats and dogs," the low-priced, unknown, small companies on the American Stock Exchange and the OTC Stocks, rather than the large firms on the NYSE.

Despite his lack of formal education, Ben was very meticulous. He read everything he could about a company he was interested in. If there was something in the balance sheet or profit-and-loss statement he didn't understand, he checked with one of his CPA customers. After a while he knew as much about accounting and taxes as anyone in the office. In addition he attended the annual meetings of many of the local companies.

When his manager leaned on him a bit and bawled him out for not buying IBM, General Motors, Philip Morris, or the like, he snapped back with, "Well, they're just too damn big. I can't get a grip on them. When is the last time you spoke to the president of IBM or the chairman of the board of General Motors? On the little companies I follow, I've talked to every president and vice president around, and, in some cases, I'm on a first-name basis. When I attended the annual meeting of DOC Optics, I was able to spend almost an hour with the chairman of the board. I can call him up any time and get an update or an explanation. Try that with your 'blue chips' "

It all fell on deaf ears, and finally Ben was told he could not buy or recommend any stock that sold below $5 and that he would have to get front office approval before he could recommend an OTC security.

Ben struggled for a while because he thought it unconscionable to recommend what he thought was mediocre and withhold advice that he believed in. He finally joined an OTC firm, that is, a member of the NASD but not a member of any exchange. Now he was free to trade in any stock he wanted, regardless of price or size.

He soon learned, however, that things were not so dif-

ferent. His new boss still wanted him to push the house recommendations and new issues. But Ben persisted in his
independence and eventually reached an accommodation
as his judgments on stock proved out.

In essence, Ben's modus operandi is simple: He seeks
out small, relatively unknown companies with small capitalization. He studies their operation, which is not too hard to
do, as such companies are not very complex. They usually
manufacture one product or provide one service in a specialized area. He makes an assessment of their future growth
vis-à-vis the current price of the stock. If he likes what he
sees, he buys a little stock and then begins to live with the
company; that is, he follows everything he can about the
company and the field it's in. He makes the acquaintance
of the president or principal stockholder (usually the same
person) by attending the annual meeting or a trade show,
or by finding a mutual friend who will introduce them, or
by a cold telephone call: "In just a few minutes of telephone
conversation I can tell whether he's a stiff, con man, or a guy
who really knows what he's doing, and I can guide myself
accordingly." As Ben gets more and more into the company, he buys more of the stock. This is a slow, careful
process.

The small capitalized company has fewer stockholders
and less stock in public hands. The purchase of a few thousand shares is often a significant trade. In many of the
companies Ben likes, fewer than a million shares are outstanding. A trade of 5,000 shares can represent 1% of all
the shares held by the public. A listed company of medium
size may have 15 to 20 million shares with the public, and
so a trade of 100,000 shares would represent less that a 1%
trade. There is also a big difference in the price. The small
OTC companies usually have low stock prices, that is, under
$10, often under $5, and sometimes even under $1 (these

are known as penny stocks). Since there is relatively little trading and, consequently, fewer traders, the spread between bid and asked price as a percentage is quite wide.

A stock traded on the NYSE in the $25 range might have a bid and asked spread of only $1/4$ point: $25 1/4$ bid and 25 asked; the spread is only 25 cents, or 1% of the price. (In 1997 the NYSE introduced spreads as low as $1/16$ in actively traded stock, and newspapers reports now reflect trade prices in sixteenths.) In Ben's kind of stock, the price would be $3 1/2$ bid and 4 offered, for a spread of $1/2$ point, or 50 cents and equal to 15% of the bid price.

There's a good reason for this. The trader who makes the market knows the demand is thin. If he sells short, he might have a tough time buying the stock back. On the other hand, if he buys, he might have trouble selling, as there is usually little interest in or visibility for the company. The trader works on his gut. His big guide is the amount of buying or selling. His first clue that something is happening is when he buys a lot of stock, even though he drops the price, or when his position is sold out and he has to go short. (See a discussion of the risks of selling short in chapter 21.)

By having a bigger spread, the trader protects himself from disaster. A spread of 20–33% is not unusual for the penny stocks. The spread may get even bigger when the trader feels he's made a mistake. For example, if his trading position is short and all the other traders are making a market of $5 1/4$ bid and $5 3/4$ asked, his market could be $5 1/4$ bid and 6 asked. He doesn't want to sell any more, but he would like to buy. If he gets worried he might raise his bid to $5 3/8$ when all the others are still $5 1/4$ to make the best bid.

The accumulation of an important position takes care and patience. It also carries risks. The position is essentially not liquid: if you need money fast, it is hard to find someone to buy your stock; in addition, small cap stocks are very hard to borrow against. Most of the small cap companies we are discussing, even though they are public, are not marginable and not bankable; that is, you could probably not use them as liquid collateral for a bank loan. So if liquidity, or bankability, is important to you, this would be a big disadvantage. Another drawback is the length of time it may take for the company to grow and be discovered. The mortality rate of a business is greatest when it is young and weak. It is also true that the rate of growth is greatest at that same time.

But Ben and his followers have found that small cap companies often pay off and can pay handsomely. He discovered a company originally called Acrylic Optics, a small chain of optometric stores, in 1975. The company had gone public in 1962 with six contact lens offices and a small contact lens manufacturing plant. As times demanded, the company changed its operation and goals. The manufacturing plant had been sold and the contact lens offices converted into full-service optometric centers offering glasses, eye examinations, contact lenses, and so on. When Ben became interested, the company consisted of twenty-five stores, sales of $5,100,000, and a dominant position in the Michigan market. The price of the stock ranged from a low bid of $7/8$ to an offer at $1 3/8$, but the stock was not easy to come by.

The total number of shares outstanding was 353,432, and the president, Dr. Donald Golden, was the principal stockholder, with 153,000. The public float was 170,000—less than 50% of the total. During the next year, the price ranged between $1 3/4$ and $3 1/2$. Ben bought between 15,000 and 20,000 shares for himself and his customers, at an average price of $2 1/4$.

As the years rolled on, some of Ben's customers sold despite his urging that they hold. Most of the time he bought the stock that they sold, and he told them he was doing this. He followed the company closely, met every important officer and employee, and occasionally called them with advice or information that might affect the company. It was a happy association.

By 1985 the company had changed its name to DOC Optics, Inc. It now had over one hundred optometric centers in five states as well as three manufacturing facilities and gross sales over $40 million per year. In the interim the stock had split 2 for 1, and 2 for 1 again, and then finally another 2 for 1. That meant Ben's 10,000 shares at a cost of perhaps $25,000 were now 80,000 shares, which hit a new high during that year of $13^1/_4$. So there was a time when, at least on paper, Ben was a millionaire.

The company had a secondary (another offering of more stock to the public) toward the end of 1985. It sold 600,000 shares in that secondary offering to the public at $10^3/_4$, most of which was bought by institutions. Although the company did not maintain its furious rate of growth after 1985, Ben still had confidence in its future and was a great booster of the stock. It had all the characteristics he looks for:

- A small company with great growth potential;
- Small capitalization (now about 2,500,000 shares outstanding;
- Low price;
- Run by owner-management (Dr. Golden's three sons were active in the business); and
- Listed on NASDAQ, the OTC computerized market and pricing system.

When the price drifted lower in 1992, DOT Optics went private; that is, the company bought back all its stock. Ben was able to cash in handsomely!

CHAPTER TWENTY

Strategy Six—Disasters and Selling Short

Harold is a retired geologist who has had a very full life. He traveled all over the world for the oil company that employed him for over thirty-five years. He searched for minerals as well as oil and gas with considerable success, and his firm was very pleased with him. It was therefore quite a shock when his company merged into a larger one and he was given the "opportunity" to retire. He had no real option, and so with some trepidation and a touch of bitterness he retired. He was still a relatively young man—just sixty. What would he do with his life? Golf and more travel were not the answer. He had suffered a permanent injury to his left leg as a young boy and had avoided sports ever since. As for travel, he had had a bellyful!

One thing he enjoyed and found very profitable was the stock market. Although his work had kept him very busy, he had always dabbled in the market. Of course, his goals were long range—no day-to-day, in-and-out trading for him. When he bought something, it was for the long pull. And now many of the seedlings were beginning to bear fruit. Why not spend his time investing and speculating and building his nest egg?

When I first met Harold and talked with him about the

market, I soon got the feeling that he was a wealthy man with a deep understanding of the market and the opportunities it offered. Recently, I asked him whether there was any technique or strategy that he found was especially good for him. He thought for a while and then got very animated. With a sparkle in his eye, he said, "Yes, indeed—disasters!" My surprised look and quizzically raised eyebrow encouraged him to continue.

"You know the market is made by people—not machines; it is not logic alone that shapes the decisions people make and the actions they take. Emotion is a powerful and uncontrollable force, which occasionally dominates reason and often results in poor decisions. That's the reason the market is generally overbought or oversold. When the public is on an emotional high, believing that the future is good, prices will be high and the market overbought. When the public is panicky about a perceived imminent recession or depression, prices are hammered down, and the market is oversold.

"The two aspects of emotion that affect the market are euphoria and panic. You often see examples of euphoria with the hot 'new issues.' The public attends exclusively to the sizzle or potential future of the new business and ignores the other factors: it's essentially a start-up; it has no history of earnings or guarantee of market; there's fantastic dilution of the stockholders' investment; there's no protection from competition from stronger and more sophisticated companies; and it has no exclusive trade secrets or patents that have been tested in the marketplace over time. The public is swept away by the dream of getting in on the ground floor.

"You see the same thing when a glamorous merger is announced or a new patent granted. The public focus is on the harvest and not on the toil and tilling needed before the harvest. People rush in and gobble up the stock, driving the price beyond all reason.

"Emotion plays the same kind of role with disasters. Panic takes over and the public sees nothing but the devastation and destruction of the catastrophe—very much like the reaction of Chicken Little when a pebble hit him in the head.

"When panic takes over, the public sells, sells, sells! They don't care about the price; it's the end! Get whatever you can—sell—soon it will be worth nothing. Of course, the price drops, and this feeds the panic, and there is more selling and more price erosion.

"You might wonder, since emotion created aberrant conditions on the upside as well as the downside, how come I only said 'disasters' when you asked how I made money in the market. Well, here's my thinking; I haven't really figured a safe way to make money when the euphoria takes over.

"Yes, I know about selling short, but that's a highly specialized game and potentially very dangerous. For example, many of the new issues open up so high, I'm sure they have to collapse. If I sell short, I'm borrowing stock to make the sale at the current high price, and then at some time thereafter, I buy and return the stock I borrowed. What if, horror of horrors, the price keeps going up? Who knows how long the delusion of the public will continue?

"And it's not only the giddy public. There's another danger. There are traders who live for the opportunity to squeeze the 'shorts.' This is usually accomplished by buying and controlling the available stock. When all the stock is controlled, they've cornered the market and can force the short seller to pay up everything he's got.

"The smaller and smaller supply of stock drives the price higher and higher, ironically, many times attracting new short sellers who think the price can't get higher than this. During the sweating time, the short seller finds that it's more and more difficult and costly to borrow the stock. Instead of a reasonable correction in the price, the stock continues to rise. It's not unusual for panic to set in on the short seller. He worries, 'When will it end? The cost of borrowing is eating me up! They're going to corner the market! I'll be wiped out! Buy the stock now! Take my loss and cover my trade.'

"Even as he makes the decision, the price keeps going up. And there's a sigh of relief when he finally buys the stock. All along he keeps remembering that old rhyme known to traders for over a hundred years': 'He who sells what isn't his'n' / Must deliver or go to prison.' "

"You know," I said to Harold, "I've seen some 'short squeezes' in my day, and they're a lot of fun if you're the spectator, but heaven help the 'shorts' involved!"

I remember one of the registered reps in our office who burst out laughing when he read a prospectus for a new issue when we were invited to join in the selling group.

"This," he howled, "is the worst piece of garbage I've ever seen. Imagine asking the public for $3 a share when the company has negative net worth and hasn't yet perfected a prototype of the equipment they're going to sell. Stay away from this deal, it's garbage all the way."

I agreed with him, and we passed on the selling group invite, but when the stock started to trade, I made the mistake of telling him that it opened at $5^1/_2$. He wouldn't believe me and checked himself. By then the market was $6^1/_4$–$6^3/_4$.

"It's an out-and-out rip-off!" he exclaimed. "I'm going to sell it short!"

Despite our admonitions, he went ahead and was exuberant when he told us that he got $8^1/_4$ when he actually made the short sale. Fortunately, he only "gambled"—

sold—100 shares short. The price kept going up, adding to his daily anxiety and to the general amusement of all the other reps.

When the stock reached $18, he groaned and announced, "That's it, you've got to be crazy to sell short! If I bought the original stock when it was $3, and then if the company crashed, that's all I would lose, $3. But in a short sale, there's no limit to my loss. That damned stock could have gone to $100, and I'd lose the whole $97 difference when I had to cover it eventually. No more shorting for me!"

"Well," Harold said, "I've never had an experience like that, and I've never shorted a stock—good instincts, I guess. But how was that possible? It obviously was a terrible stock. How could it keep going up like that?"

In retrospect it is easy to explain. In a free market, price is determined by supply and demand. As the price goes up, more sellers are willing to sell, and then the supply meets the demand and the price settles down. But when you have a new issue, there is a very finite or limited supply—only the number of shares being offered for sale.

In the foregoing example, this deal was so bad that the issuer quickly realized it would not be sold, just as our rep had surmised, so the issuer placed the stock in friendly hands temporarily. The deal was closed, and trading on the stock opened at a premium. It didn't take too many trades to get the price to $6, double the original price, since there was very little stock offered in the new issue, and most of that stock was controlled by friendly hands.

The inflated price, of course, attracted attention, especially from many of those who thought the stock was garbage and totally overpriced. Many became short sellers, trying to make a quick profit because they assumed the price would collapse soon. As the price continued to rise because it was completely controlled, more short sellers were attracted to the stock, but there still was no supply. There was finally a settlement after threats of lawsuits and SEC investigations. A costly lesson for the naïve and those looking to get rich quick.

So how does Harold make money out of disasters? He explained his strategy to me this way:

"It's just that when there's a disaster, people panic. They misperceive the effect of the terrible event. If you keep your head and are able to make a realistic assessment of the damage, you can buy things below their true value. Here is a good example.

"Remember a couple of years ago, there was a rumor that cellular phones caused cancer of the brain. It all started with a lawsuit in Florida against NEL Corp., a unit of a giant Japanese electronics company and GTE Mobilnet. This lawsuit claimed that a woman had developed cancer by using a portable cellular phone and later died. The price of all cellular stocks started to decline, and the industry lost millions of dollars in market value. The manufacturer and industry association held press conferences to deny the allegations. Of course, this attracted more attention and more panic and more selling.

"Needless to say, there were some stock analysts anxious to grab a quick headline. They jumped in and urged their followers to sell because, as they said, 'Even if it's not true, there will be dozens of lawsuits. The expense of the trials and the harsh publicity will kill sales and the whole industry.'

"All this time, cellular phones were selling at double-digit rates; they were adding seventy-six hundred customers a day to the mobile systems, and this was the hottest industry around. When the stocks all dropped between 15 and 20% in about a week of panic and bad press, I bought shares in each of the leading companies. They were a steal, the market had overreacted. And when the prices corrected themselves. I was sitting pretty.

"Another example: Most people will remember the crash of October 19, 1987. The Dow Jones averages dropped over 500 points in one day, at a time when 500 points represented almost 25% of the total Dow Jones averages. It was the greatest crash since 1929 and in some ways even more dramatic—never had prices dropped so far in a single day!

"It all started with heavy selling and weakened prices, which triggered an institutional investment strategy known as portfolio insurance. The basic idea was that institutions could lock in profits by selling stock index futures contracts as prices fell. This didn't start the crash, but it certainly helped it along. The market simply could not handle the volume. The usual practice of dropping the price to stop selling did not work. They kept selling. Panic had set in, and, as wider and wider circles of investors became aware of what was happening, there was more and more selling. Only the close of the market at 4:00 P.M. stopped the hemorrhage.

"I must admit I was shook up, too," Harold went on to say. "But as I checked my portfolio, there was nothing I wanted to dump at the prices then available. As things started to settle the next day or so, I began to think the stocks I liked were a better buy than a sell. I began to nibble at stocks usually too high for me, but now bargains. Some of them have tripled and quadrupled in the ten years since 'the great disaster of '87.' As a matter of fact, we've had a bull market for the ten years since 1987, and I don't see it ending in the near future."

The exciting ride in the market in the fall of 1997 convinced many people that it is a good time to hold or to buy when the market takes a large drop. Those who held on or bought through the volatile market days in October and November 1997 were a lot happier than those who sold in panic or too soon.

Whenever you have a panic—regardless of the cause— the reason and good judgment of the public is suspended. Unbridled emotion takes over, and there is chaos in the market. Opportunities abound for the realist.

CHAPTER TWENTY-ONE

Strategy Seven—Convertible Debentures

Many years ago, just home from work, I was startled to learn that my darling daughter had been called to the principal's office. She was an excellent student, very well behaved.

"What happened?" I asked. "Why were you sent to the principal's office?"

"It was because of show and tell," she explained. At that time, each child demonstrated or explained some special skill or experience to the class and then answered any questions. Each child was given a turn, and there was a great competition to "show and tell" about something the others were unacquainted with.

When my daughter's turn came, she gave a short talk on the advantages of the convertible debenture! She was eight years old! The teacher was dumbstruck; she had never heard of a convertible debenture and asked her to write the phrase on the blackboard. After lunch several of the teachers from neighboring classrooms dropped by to look at the board. By three o'clock the summons came from the principal's office. When the two were alone, the principal asked, "Now, my dear, what's a convertible debenture?"

How she explained it, I'll never know, but I did know

that she understood all about convertibles. She started to learn about the stock market and public companies when she learned how to play Monopoly at age five. Understanding that the convertible debenture was the ideal security came easy.

A bond or debenture is a debt of the corporation and must be repaid according to its terms. It carries a fixed rate of interest, paid quarterly or semiannually—unlike a dividend on common stock, which may or may not be paid depending on the profit earned that year and actions taken by the board of directors. The debenture holder gets his or her money back and the regular periodic payment of interest. The holder, like other creditors, takes precedence over the stockholders when a company is in liquidation. Debenture holders usually don't take precedence over bank debt.

The debenture holder, however, does not share in any great prosperity of the company. If the business grows, the value of the company and its stock shares can double or triple in value, and the dividend on common stock can grow into an important return. But the debenture stands still; its value remains the same. It is a specific debt, and when the time comes, it will be paid off.

In order to raise money by debenture or bond, the corporation must offer an interest rate high enough to attract lenders. There's never a shortage of people and enterprises that need money, and they compete with another for capital. The bargaining chip is the interest rate. Of course, the strength of the borrower is an important factor, as are the length of time and the subordinate position of the debt relative to other corporate debts.

Very often the interest rate necessary to get the loan makes it economically unfeasible for the company. That's when the convertible feature comes into play. In a convertible debenture, the holder is given the option of converting the debt into common stock at a preset price. As the company becomes successful and the value of its stock rises, the convertible debenture holder has an opportunity to make an impressive profit by converting the debenture into common stock. Thus the convertible debenture becomes a very attractive security, as the holder can elect to be either a creditor or a partner.

The need for a high interest rate drops when the feature of convertibility is added, and it becomes easier for the corporation to raise the money it needs. The conversion price is usually set 20% to 30% above the current price of the common stock, with interest at a relatively low rate. For example, the convertible debenture is usually issued in denominations of $1,000, with interest, for example, at 6% for 20 years, payable semiannually. At the time of issue, the common stock may trade at $8. If the conversion price is $10 (i.e. 25% above the common stock price), each debenture could be converted into 100 shares of stock. As the company prospers and the common stock goes to $15, the convertible debenture will trade at about $150 (i.e., $1,500 bonds and debentures are quoted less that last digit). A bid of 95 and an asked of 97 means $950 bid and $975 offered.

The new capital is put to work and often results in better performance by the corporation. The lower interest paid for the money helps, too, and profit grows. Soon the price of the common stock reacts and goes up. The holder of a convertible debenture can sit tight and wait to decide which way she wants to go.

The terms are spelled out in the security, and there is usually a term of years during which the holder can elect to convert. If the holder is not ready to sell out and take the profit, it may pay to forestall conversion and continue to collect the interest while waiting to see how the company will fare. There are times when the business falters, loses money, and the price of the common stock goes down. How much better then to be a creditor than a stockholder! Even if the company does well and the price of the common stock continues to rise above the conversion price, it may pay to put off conversion. The common stock may pay no dividend as management decides to plow profits back into the company for more growth. Interest on the debenture, however, continues, and the holder collects it until she converts. Of course, during this time the price of the convertible debenture continues to rise to reflect its true value.

There is no need to convert immediately. When, however, the dividend on the common stock increases to the point where it is substantially higher than the interest earned by the bond, it may be time to convert. For example, 6% interest on $1,000 is $60. If the dividend on the common stock is raised to $1 per share, conversion results in 100 shares and $100 in dividends—tempting. Of course, the company could decrease its dividend the next year! You may decide that the increase in yield is worth the risk of becoming a shareholder rather than a creditor.

There is another aspect to consider: the commission on the sale. Commissions on bonds are usually a flat fee, regardless of price, that is, $5 or $10 per bond, even if the price is $1,500. Commissions on stock are usually determined by the price of the stock and are considerably higher. There are some times when you can do better by selling the bonds than by converting them and selling the stock. A buyer may be willing to pay more for a convertible debenture than the stock it can be converted to. (Also, on the sale of a bond you get the interest accumulated to that date). A bond is also more acceptable as collateral than is common stock, and if you hope to borrow money, this could be an important factor in deciding whether to convert.

All in all, the convertible debenture is the dream security. Ironically, most Wall Street investors do not own any. These debentures are usually issued when a company is having trouble raising inexpensive money. To "do a secondary," that is, to sell additional common stock to the public, the sale would have to be at a price below the current trading price—a bargain—or else, why would the public buy? On the other hand, the strike, or conversion, price of a convertible debenture is usually set at least 20% higher than the current trading price. So, in effect, when a convertible debenture is sold and the security ends up as a common stock, it will be at a price at least 20% higher than the company could get at the time of the issue. For many investors the issue and sale of a convertible is a sign of weakness, and they stay away from the company.

Another reason for public unawareness is the commission. As indicated earlier, there is a disincentive for brokers to recommend convertible debentures. After the original issue, the commissions are ridiculously low for the money involved in the sale, very few investors trade their convertibles, and the money is usually locked up for a long time. Thus, brokers don't push convertibles.

Betty, a quiet millionaire I know, learned about convertible debentures by accident; as she began to understand them, she more or less made them her investment life. As a single woman in her late thirties with no other special skills than an ability to do simple bookkeeping, her investments were very conservative. They were her protection and security for retirement, and she didn't like to take chances. She bought preferred stocks; she liked their regular dividends and the preferences of payment in case of liquidation.

Then one day the management of a company in which she owned 100 preferred shares woke up to the fact that the dividends paid on the preferred shares were an accounting expense after taxes. The company paid approximately 40 cents in taxes on each dollar of profit and then had to pay the preferred dividend for the money left. By exchanging the preferred for a debenture or bond, the interest on the bond would become an expense before taxes, because a bond is a debt and interest thereon an expense. The profit would be smaller, thus resulting in less tax, and therefore greater cash flow for the corporation and more benefit to stockholders.

In order for the preferred stockholders to agree to the exchange, management made the bond convertible into the common stock at a reasonable strike price (just above the price at which the common stock traded), with interest at 6%, the same as that earned by the preferred stock. Once this was accomplished, the interest of 6% paid on the bonds was deducted as expense, and only the balance was taxable. It left the company with more capital for expansion, growth, or dividends for the common stock.

Betty liked the result. She received the same money— now called interest instead of dividends—and the company was in better shape to survive. Since the company was a small cap and relatively unknown, there wasn't much of a market for the new convertible debentures. As the price drifted lower, Betty was quick to realize that, at the lower price, the interest paid actually gave her an 8% return.

The quarterly reports indicated that, with the help of the money saved, the company had started to turn around. Betty bought more debentures—but very carefully—only a few at a time and rarely at the offered price. As she seemed to be the only buyer, the price drifted lower, and she was shocked one day to realize that 40% of her total capital was tied up in those debentures. When she decided to sell half, she learned a very valuable lesson: there were no buyers! They bought the first five or ten bonds at the bid price, but then the bid price really dropped, and she learned that even at that ridiculous price, buyers wouldn't take many bonds.

One of the brokers who made a market even called her to ask what was the matter: "Why are you selling like that? Is the company going broke?"

She denied any special knowledge and, after thinking it over for a while, recognized that she had started a minor panic in the company's securities. This course of events resulted in her determination to find out how she really stood, and she began an intensive, almost panicky, analysis of the company. To her pleasant surprise, everything was pretty much status quo—more money was being spent on advertising, which resulted in a bigger share of market; profit margins were steady; debt was being reduced.

"Why am I selling? What's the panic?" she wondered, "Interest at the current low price is over 12%, and the company is in better shape to pay it than ever before. What's so terrible about investing 40% or even 50% of my capital in a good thing? It was not so long ago I had all my money in a savings and loan, and many of them exploded like popcorn! I like this company. They give good reports and I can see what's going on. Besides, even if they, God forbid, go broke, I'm still a creditor."

Betty then started to pick up additional bonds at the new low price, and, ironically, there were more of them for sale than before. Betty held on to her convertibles for several years, at a terrific interest rate which provided her with fresh capital for investment. Eventually, the company turned around and scored big. As the price of the common stock rose with each quarterly report, the strike price for converting into common stock was quickly passed. The common stock doubled and doubled again. The price of the bonds soared, too, but Betty would never sell. She finally gave up her beloved bonds when the company merged with a much larger one in exchange for common stock in the new company.

Betty computed that the growth of her investment, exclusive of the interest, had been over 1,000%. She's now the most knowledgeable stockholder I know on the subject of convertibles, and, of course, she's always looking for and accumulating new convertible debenture issues that meet her criteria. She's a quiet millionaire if ever I knew one!

Here are a few convertible debenture examples:

1. **Acrylic Optic Corp.** went public in 1961, offering common stock at $1.25 per share and convertible debentures paying 6% interest and convertible into common stock at $1.50, i.e., 666²/₃ shares of common stock for each bond. The underwriters set it up that way so the investors would get at least 6% on their money while waiting for the chain of contact lens offices to grow. Total sales were less than $500,000 per year, at the time, so the $300,000 raised when the company went public was an important shot in the arm.

It was a very small company, and there was very little Wall Street interest. Competition in the contact lens field was growing and the company's use of radio and TV was copied by many of its competitors.

Then the company made an important change in operations by launching full-service optometric stores in two locations, with special attention to store appearance and an extensive choice of frames and glasses. The new approach was successful but slow to show results on the financials. The stock floated down to ⁵/₈ bid, ⁷/₈ offered and traded only by appointment.

The bonds were no better—not much of a market and a big spread, i.e., 75 bid, 85 offered. This meant for a $1,000 bond, the market maker would pay $750 or would sell it for $850—the "spread," or difference, being $100— not a very attractive market. (Incidentally, when you buy a bond you add the accumulated interest to the price.) One bondholder with ten bonds called the president of the company and offered to sell at 80 and was politely but firmly turned down.

As time passed, the new format resulted in dramatic profits, and the price of the common began to move up, as did the price of the bonds. To create a better climate for trading, the stock was split 2 for 1; a year or so later, it was split 2 for 1 again, and finally 2 for 1 a third time. Thus an original share of stock became eight shares and each share ultimately traded in the teens. During this time, the bond was called, but the $1,000 convertible bond had traded at a high of $18,000. Of course, everyone converted into the common stock because, for example, 666.66 shares had split to 5,333.28 shares. Later, when the common stock traded at $15, the original investment of $1,000 was worth $80,000.

The pot of gold hidden in convertible debentures is not always due to a sensational jump in the price of the common stock, however. There can be excellent returns in just the action of the bonds.

2. **Zenith Electric,** traded on the New York Stock Exchange, had a convertible bond with a $6^1/_4\%$ interest rate. The corporation had a series of losses, which at one point in 1991 drove the price of the common stock down to $5, and the convertible, with a strike price of $38, dropped to a low of $35 (i.e., $350 for a $1,000 bond). With interest at $6^1/_4\%$, if the bonds continued to pay, the yield would be close to 18%.

A short time thereafter, a Korean firm made a very large investment in Zenith Electric, practically ensuring the continuation of operations and probable payment of regular interest on the bonds. The bonds then shot up to 70, even though the strike price was still a long way from where the common stock was trading. Although the common stock may never get close to the conversion price, the yield to maturity on the Zenith bond in 2011 will be over 20% per year, since each bond is redeemed for $1,000 on maturity. Not too shabby a return over a twenty-year span.

3. **Pogo Producing**, traded on the NYSE, is an oil and gas exploration company. Its common stock bounced

around and at one time was as low as $2^1/_2$. In 1990, however, the common traded at 4 and the 8% convertible of 2005 was selling at 60, because the strike price was far away at $39.50.

In the mid-1990s the price of natural gas increased and some of the exploration began to pay off. The common stock kept rising and in June 1996 hit a high of 38. The company called the bonds at 102, as it had a right to do, and as of July 15, 1996, the yield on the 8% bonds bought at 60 would have been over 20% per year for the six-year period.

You can see why the convertible bond is the ideal security for the individual investor. It can fulfill your dream of getting rich, with multiples of ten or even twenty times your original investment as a stockholder and, at the same time, enable you to sleep peacefully as a creditor.

CHAPTER TWENTY-TWO

Strategy Eight—New Issues (IPO's)

New issues (also called initial public offerings or IPO's) afford great opportunities for the savvy investor, because the company going public and the underwriter will probably offer the issue at a bargain price.

The basic objective of an IPO is to sell a piece of the company by selling a block of stock to the public, thereby creating new capital. A sale to the "public," rather than to individuals or venture capital groups, creates a public market for the stock that will continue in the future. The company ends up with many stockholders rather than a few "partners." Each stockholder owns a relatively small share of the company and therefore has some interest in its welfare and success, but not enough to warrant interference with management of the company.

A significant result of going public is that the market produces a piece for the stock. "Buyers" and "sellers" determine the price by the actions they take. The greater the number of stockholders, the greater the stability of the stock, as there is a greater pool of potential sellers and buyers. Actually, stockholders are often buyers rather than sellers because they want to accumulate a larger share of the company. When there are many buyers and sellers, the price will not soar or fall precipitously when a few hundred thousand shares are traded.

For example, Cisco Systems, Inc., has over 690 million shares outstanding. On a fairly typical day in the nineties it could trade over ten million shares with less than a point of fluctuation.

Price and "value," although closely related, are different, however. "Price" is what a willing and able buyer is ready to pay and a seller is willing to accept at any given time. "Value" lies in the eye of the beholder: it is what someone thinks a stock is or will be worth in the future. The balance sheet of a business may indicate a negligible net worth, but its potential may be worth billions.

If, for example, a corporation spends almost all its capital on research and finally discovers a cure for cancer, the price of that stock after the cure is announced will be determined by what buyers believe the future will bring rather than by its balance sheet net worth. Cisco Systems, Inc. was trading in June 1997 for about $65 per share; the book value per share was $5.19.

A very popular and useful yardstick for the price of the stock is the P/E (price/earnings) ratio, which is expressed as the current price of the common stock divided by the earnings per share in the past year.

$$P/E = \frac{\text{Current price}}{\text{Earnings/share/year}}$$

If a stock trades at $15 and the earnings were $1.50 in the past year, then the P/E ratio is 10 (15/1.5 = 10). Interestingly, the range of P/E ratios for publically traded stocks can range from a low of 5 or 6 to a high of 50 or more, thus reflecting what the market thinks about the future of the company and its stock.

When a company contemplates an initial sale of the stock, the critical problem is centered on how to price the original offering. Of course, the company would like to get as much as possible; however, since there are often no significant earnings per share in the new issue's history, the P/E ratio is primarily driven by anticipation. Thus there is wide latitude in setting the price. The company finalizes the price when the SEC advises that the offering is effective and the shares may be sold.

The "red herring" (a preliminary prospectus that is used to alert the public and create interest in the deal; cautionary language is printed in red on the cover) gives a proposed range for the price of the stock, e.g., "between $6–$8 per share." This is done so potential buyers get some idea of what the price will be in order to decide whether they want to buy the stock. There is no requirement that this range remain fixed. The company is free to raise or lower the final price. When there is an overwhelming demand for the stock, the company may believe it has priced the stock too low and adjust it higher. On the other hand, when the underwriter reports little or no interest in the stock, the price is often dropped, in an effort to attract buyers. On occasion, the price may be dropped several times.

Raising capital by the offering of stock to the public is a vital Wall Street function. It provides an important opportunity for small investors and the public to invest in a business. The rules and laws for how this should be done are set forth in great detail by the Securities and Exchange Commission.

When shares are to be offered to the public, they must be accompanied by a prospectus in which full disclosure of the corporation's history, its business, management, ownership background, and certified (audited) financials are set forth in detail. All of this must be revealed to the satisfaction of the SEC as must a list of the potential risks and dangers involved in buying the shares of this particular corporation and any private transactions made prior to this offering that might have a bearing on the company's future management or its stock.

The prospectus for a new issue is a detailed presentation of the company and its securities. By and large, this aspect of the "going public" process is closely supervised by the SEC. As a result, the average private investor has an opportunity to learn more about the company than he ever could by his own investigation. An investor who studies the prospectus can make an intelligent decision about whether he should buy the stock at the price offered.

The prospectus that convinces you to buy the stock carries the same message to thousands of other investors, registered reps, financial advisors, and so on. And the orders and "expression of intent" often make the proposed offering a "hot issue." The better the deal, the greater the demand, and the weaker the chances of getting any stock at the offering price. The conventional wisdom among the cognoscenti is, "If it's a new issue I can get, I don't want it. It must be a bomb." If the demand for a new issue is many times the quantity being offered, you can't give everyone all they want. The lucky buyer and the number of shares he gets is determined by the underwriters. And believe me, it's not by luck!

When you have greater demand than supply, the price goes up; when supply is greater than demand, the price goes down. In a free market, price usually fluctuates with demand and supply.

When there is a "hot" new issue, everyone knows that the demand is greater than the supply; therefore, the price will go up once it starts to trade. No one knows this better than the underwriter. How much it will go up is a function of the demand and the limited (and often controlled) supply. Allocation of the new stock gives the underwriter the power of Santa Claus. Who will get these goodies? The ones who can do him the most good, of course: large institutional firms that do important business with him; other underwriters who will return the favor; brokers who create big commissions all get shares to be passed on to their favorite customers and buyers who will hold the stock until needed. The history of new issues is studded with examples of stock that opened up 20%, 50% or 100% or more higher than the offering price. When there's a steaming market for an initial public stock offering, suddenly the small investor can't get any stock.

Here are three impressive examples that are representative of the wild action during the up phase of the new issue or "going public" cycle:

> **Boston Chicken, Inc.,** a rotisserie chicken restaurant chain, doubled in the first hour of trading after its initial public offering. Originally offered at $20 on November 9, 1993, it traded as high as $48 on the first day of trading and higher in the months that followed.

> **Netscape Communications Corp.** is a provider client and server software company that links people and information over the Internet. In August 1995, ten million shares were offered at $14 and traded at $28 the first day. By 1996 the company had traded over thirteen million shares at $58^1/_2$, after jumping to a high of $75.

> **Yahoo! Inc.** is an Internet company that offers a network of globally branded properties and specialty programming. This popular Internet search engine helps surfers find sites on the Web. Offered on April 12, 1996, at $13 a share, it traded as high as $43 on the first day.

CHAPTER TWENTY-THREE

Strategy Nine—Know the People

Every so often the final decision about whether you should buy a stock comes down to what kind of people manage and control the firm. The industry and the products may be fine, the balance sheet and promise of growth excellent, but if management or controlling ownership lacks integrity, stay away. There are individuals who twist and turn every business to their personal advantage, who think the only thing that matters in business is to feather their own nests. They view the public corporation as their personal property. They consider the dividends that the stockholders sometimes receive to be a gift.

Outrageous behavior by some management is almost beyond belief—private jets, multiple homes in exotic places, mistresses, personal bodyguards, private railroad cars, art collections, an entourage of friends and relatives on the company payroll, and so on. Such perks have all surfaced at some time or another when a scandal has broken. But most of the time, the scoundrels keep their greed well hidden. What to do?

Well, there are some clues. Greed is like athletic ability: its lack can't be completely hidden. In the annual statements the stockholders are told the salaries of officers and directors, as well as the number and price of options awarded to each. When the president and possibly other officers award themselves million-dollar salaries or raises, huge stock options, or other perks and the company has barely broken even—or perhaps has lost money—you must ask why. Yes, it is possible that they earned their money, even though the company lost money, but this would happen only in highly unusual circumstances. You must ask yourself if they would command those salaries and perks if they were working for a private enterprise or for anyone else. In most cases, people evaluate themselves through the end of the telescope that magnifies, and since management usually controls salaries and perks, the boys can be very good to themselves. (And yes, it is usually the boys—the corporate girls normally don't get to take home the prizes at this level.) It's amazing how management (the CEO, president, chairman of the board, or director), which already controls—and sometimes even owns a majority of the shares—can be awarded the lion's share of sweetheart options on the premise that the option provides an incentive for it to do better.

If you are a stockholder in such a company, you'll find there is little you can do. Your protests will be ignored, your vote on the annual proxy statement will not carry, and you will be stonewalled if you attend the annual meeting, where such perks are voted on. Should you resort to legal action, the cost will be borne by you unless you win, whereas management has all the resources of the corporation to use against you. In addition, this kind of case is difficult to win because the burden of proof is on you to prove that the salary and perks are excessive. Generally, the activities of the Board of Directors are deemed to be in good faith in the regular course of business; for example, directors are thought to have used their best judgment in arriving at fair salaries and perks.

As a practical matter, when you come to the conclusion that management is rapacious and overreaching, avoid the company; if you have already invested, sell at a propitious opportunity. There are many other more worthy places to put your money.

On the other side of the "know the people" strategy is investing by "looking for the good guys." A friend says, "I only invest in companies in one industry, the one I'm in. I know a lot of people in it, have worked for some of the best, and have been on industry panels, tradeshow committees, and charity events with others. I know the kinds of good products they have introduced in the past, and I know how they get the most from their employees. I even know when they have made significant contributions in time or money to their communities.

"When I know someone is really smart and honest and has a great track record, I follow his career and I invest in the company he goes to next—if he has a chance to run it or to turn it around. I've never lost money by following the good guys, and when they leave a company for what I suspect is a private disagreement with other powerful management, I usually sell. My compelling reason is that I no longer have the reason I went into it, and I suspect that things will not go as well without 'my guy' there in the future. I've seldom been wrong so far. And even if the stock didn't go up or down a lot as I followed the honest guy, I still felt good about where I had my money and why."

CHAPTER TWENTY-FOUR

Strategy Ten—The Quarterback Connection

Paul is a young man in his late twenties and has all the credentials for making a success on Wall Street. He earned an MBA at a prestigious university, where he was trained to handle financial matters. Because he was schooled in the interpretation of balance sheets and at home with the most sophisticated computers, everyone expected him to shine on Wall Street, and he was entrusted with the family money.

After three years of picking and choosing, buying and selling, hedging and shopping, he came to the sickening realization that he wasn't doing very well. In fact, he hadn't even done as well as the Dow Jones averages. The great confidence he had in the special knowledge he had acquired in business school was shaken. So much that he "knew" wasn't so. The rules weren't always followed; cause and effect weren't in play; you rarely had all the facts. Why should a drop in the unemployment figures be bad news for Wall Street? Or cutting off Iraqi oil be good for the Dow Jones averages? It really didn't matter that it be logical, the important thing was to come down on the right side, to end up making investments that made money.

Then Paul had an investment epiphany, which he calls his "quarterback connection." He explains it this way:

"I can check out a balance sheet and make a reasonable judgment of how a corporation is doing and will probably keep doing—but I can't know when there's going to be a great change in operations for the better, or when they're going on an acquisitions binge, or planning to reorganize the corporate structure, so that 2 + 2 will equal 7. These things happen only when there's great new leadership by people who have real business savvy and the incentive to make things happen. I don't mean just a change in president or CEO, who are essentially employee caretakers or administrators. They can make the wheel go smoother and more economically, but they rarely make the changes that result in major price moves in the stock.

"I look for new 'quarterbacks'—guys or gals who call the signals and select the plays—they're usually people with substantial new investment money in the company, their own or that of a financial group they represent. This comes about when there's been a struggle for control, a reorganization after bankruptcy, or a sale of control or shift by realignment, and a new player calls the shots. A change in quarterbacks augurs well for some change in the company, but that does not mean it will always be better. Sometimes you get more of the same or something worse. Action doesn't always mean improvement. There are quarterbacks and quarterbacks, and some have proven themselves to be stars. They deliver and so I look for them just as avidly as I look for the "sleeper" company everyone has overlooked.

"When a great quarterback enters the game, I feel that he knows a lot more about what's going on than I do. He's putting his own money in the deal, usually a substantial stake, and his friends and financial partners are doing the same. They don't go into the deal to make 10% on their money. They see an opportunity for many multiples of their capital over time. This is not a quick-buck crowd—they're content to see the game played out, and the quarterback is not in there for the perks. Often the new signal caller doesn't even take a title; he doesn't need the trappings; he knows who's boss.

"How do I find these great movers and shakers? I just read the newspapers and magazines. The changes in control of public companies are reported in some detail, and there's usually a profile of the business background of the key figures. It's like a form sheet at the racetrack. What races did they participate in before and who won?

"Of course, I don't follow blindly. I check out the company myself and decide whether it's an investment opportunity for me. I also try to compare what the new boss is paying for the stock to what I have to pay to get in on the deal. Sometimes they get such a good deal that I think it's crazy for me to buy in, and other times the stock is trading at even less than the new control group paid. At this point I start to nibble away, and as time goes on I have a chance to observe the new management in action. If I like what I see, I accumulate a bigger position.

"Strangely, on several occasions the stock actually dropped after the change in control. I guess some of the original shareholders didn't want to take a chance on the new management. And perhaps some sold out of a sense of loyalty to the old group or because they no longer had a business reason for owning the stock—you know, friend of management, the financial advisors, insurance firms, travel agents, former suppliers, etc. Plus all the employees who had stock in the company when they were fired by the new management may no longer want to have anything to do with a stock controlled by the guys who fired them!

"Once I've decided I like the new quarterback, I don't let the drop in price scare me. I buy more. This is a great chance to build a real stake, although it can get nerve-racking if the price keeps dropping. There are several situations that are still in play, and time will tell how right or wrong I am."

Paul did very well with the following companies:

California Federal Bank

In March 1994, California Federal Bank came out with a Rights Offering of 21,642,110 shares at $9 per share. Each stockholder was given one Right for every 1.5 shares of common stock held and the further privilege of oversubscribing at the same price for shares not picked up by other stockholders. The Rights were traded on the NYSE, and anyone who wanted to buy the stock could buy the Rights and subscribe.

There was a standby purchase agreement with institutional and individual investors to buy up to 16,647,777 of any shares not subscribed for and a guarantee that they would get at least 4,994,333 shares. The last reported sale of the stock on February 28, 1994, was 11 1/4. Rights were scheduled to expire on November 16, 1994.

The list of standby purchasers was impressive—some of the most sophisticated financial people in the Street—with Michael Price and his Heine Securities Corp. and Merrill Lynch Asset Management among the leaders. Together the group had agreed to invest over $150,000,000 in the company if needed, provided the standby investors would invest at least $50,000,000 if the stockholders took all they could. The Rights Offering was successfully completed in 1994.

The bank and the stock did well, and in the summer of 1996 all the stock was bought by another bank at approximately $24 a share, plus a possible kicker in money to be recovered from the federal government. In effect, the standby agreement created a new quarterback in the group of standby players.

Telemundo

Telemundo Group, Inc., a Spanish-language broadcaster that at one time reached 86% of all U.S. Hispanic households, filed for Chapter 11 bankruptcy protection in July 1993. At the end of 1994, the company emerged with a court-approved reorganization plan. Outstanding debt had been reduced from $300 million to $117 million and the current stockholders were wiped out. Control was acquired by Leon Black and his Apollo Group. Black had masterminded several other bankruptcy court takeovers, for example, Interco, Inc., and Gillette Holdings, Inc. Although he owned only 15% of the common stock, other stockholders aligned with him to gave him de facto control.

In February 1995 Nugget Partners L.P., run by Arthur Goldberg, lifted its share in Telemundo to 11.2%. The price went from $7.31 to $15.62 per share. Under the new quarterbacks, the company's stock hemmed and hawed, but on March 10, 1998, it was selling at $41.25. Later that year, Telemundo was taken over at $44.25 per share.

CHAPTER TWENTY-FIVE

Strategy Eleven—Know When to Hold 'Em

Two years after starting this book and recording the tactics and financial techniques of the quiet millionaires who had crossed my path, I was thrilled to read a feature story in the *New York Times* in December of 1995. The headline read: "A Quiet Auditor Leaves Yeshiva a Fortune."

Anne Schreiber, who lived in a rent-stabilized studio apartment in New York City, died at the age of 101. She had retired from her job with the IRS in 1944, never having earned more than $4,000 a year. She carefully invested her savings of $5,000 in the stock market. Over the next half century, she parlayed that $5,000 into an estate worth about $22 million. Her holdings included shares in Coca-Cola, Paramount, Schering-Plough, and over one hundred other public companies.

She took her investment career seriously, analyzing annual statements, management philosophy, product and service quality. Her investment strategies were simple: forget about market highs and lows at any particular time; reinvest your dividends; hang tough and seldom sell. "She never looked for a quick buck," her broker said. "Her whole idea was to get performance on a long-term basis. Over the long run she felt the value would grow."

Her lawyer observed, "You think Warren Buffet was good at this sort of thing? She ran rings around Warren Buffet."

Ms. Schreiber had known tough times as a child in Brooklyn. Her father died young and her mother sold real estate to support the family. She went to secretarial school and landed a bookkeeper's job. After law school in Washington, D.C., she joined the Internal Revenue Service as an estate auditor. Although her work was outstanding, she never got a promotion and felt that women were shortchanged.

In a handwritten letter in which she outlined her life, she stated her desire to give nearly all her fortune of $22,000,000 to Yeshiva University to help women and middle-class families with tuition. She had never attended Yeshiva, and no one at that university had ever heard of her.

This story is especially dear to me because she used the techniques I believe are so important. These were her steps in her strategy:

1. Check out the company carefully.
2. Act when you're happy with its services, products, and management; when you are confident that you are buying the stock at a fair price; and when you feel optimistic about the company's future.
3. Reinvest the dividends.
4. Sit back and give the stock a chance to grow. The secret lies in long-term appreciation.

If I had to give one maxim, this is it—

NEVER SELL UNLESS YOU HAVE A COMPELLING REASON!

If you have chosen carefully (good products, good management, industry with a good future), the company will prosper, and its stock will continue to grow unless there is a major change in the company, for example, a management shakeup, a merger or large acquisition, a hostile takeover, or a shift in the competitive environment that causes it to slow down. The ability to recognize such changes makes more millionaires than the ability to find great opportunities.

There are hundreds of books and thousands of magazine articles advising how to find and buy stocks with a potential for profit. Unfortunately, I've never found one with the secrets for successful selling. At best they offer guidelines or formulas for defending your profit and capital by liquidating your position: "Put a stop-loss sell order at 20% below the current price"; or "When it reaches your target price, get out"; or "If it trades at a P/E ratio of over 20, then sell on the news."

There are circumstances when each of the above guidelines makes sense for an appropriate action, but I've learned the hard way that selling by formula often results in financial tragedy. There is nothing so sad as buying a stock after long and careful analysis, nursing it over time, enjoying its move up 20% or so, and then, by applying one of the suggested formulas (stop-loss, for example), you sell out to protect that 20% profit, only to watch the stock go on to double and triple your original price. The old adage "You'll never go broke taking a profit" is cold comfort when the stock you sold goes to the moon.

You may be thinking, Why can't someone buy the stock back if it's so good, or just pick another stock? First, it's not so easy to find the elephants—those great big winners—the young IBMs, Microsofts, Xeroxes, and so on. There are sure to be many great opportunities in your lifetime, but, alas, it can be years before you recognize that you have an elephant. So selling is very serious business. And, once you've sold a stock, it is very hard psychologically to buy it back at a higher price. When you do, you are essentially admitting that you made a mistake; this is hard for many people to admit, even if it's only to yourself. It gets harder as the price goes higher and your sale of that great stock seems dumber and dumber. You keep waiting for the next dip in price, but it never seems to come.

So when you find a company you really like, it may start out as just another casual date. As time goes on, you may find that your affection strengthens, and then what you have ripens into a relationship. With confidence in your future together, you're going steady! Periodic changes in what is stylish or popular should not break you up. You're committed. Despite the hallowed and much-quoted admonition, "Don't fall in love with a stock," there are companies that warrant " 'til death do us part" commitments—like those Ms. Schreiber had.

On the other hand, anyone who is active in the market for a while will have no trouble finding examples of having held too long. In hindsight they will support the warning, "Don't fall in love with a stock." By holding too long, you may indeed end up making less profit than if you had sold at the top, or perhaps you may end up with a partial loss—or even a total loss of your original investment.

Nevertheless, more money is lost by selling too soon and missing the dream. Finding and holding onto an emerging monster, a real elephant, can make the difference in the quality of life for you and your whole family. See Part III for examples of some of these long-haul performers.

CHAPTER TWENTY-SIX

Strategy Twelve—
A Margin Account

There are some stocks that should be held for generations, passed on to the children and grandchildren like heirlooms. But passing on the stock is not enough; your beneficiaries must understand why the company is great and why the stock should be held. One of the advantages of passing stock on to the next generation is the current tax law. It provides beneficiaries with a new tax base. That is, your heirs get to start with the value of your stock at the time of your death as their "original" price. So neither your estate nor your heirs have to pay capital gains taxes on the gains you made from the time you bought the stock until the date you died. When your heirs eventually sell the stock, the capital gains tax for them is levied only on the profit they made resulting from the rise in price after your death. The stepped-up tax base provides substantial savings in taxes as the stock is sold in succeeding generations. On the other hand, the price of the stock at your death, rather than its original cost, is reflected in your total net worth at death and is subject to estate taxes.

It is interesting to speculate that some of America's greatest family fortunes have resulted from generation after generation's holding onto stock and growing with the companies. When there is a large, valuable block of stock, it is easy to borrow capital against it for further investment without selling any of the old family stock. Valuable stocks provide a platform for the next generation's lives. Often the expanding dividends alone can provide for a comfortable lifestyle.

Ah, you might think, what's the use of dreaming— finding the right stock and holding it for generations? That's just spinning my wheels? You want to make it now, and make some improvements in your own life. Well, as the Chinese say, "a journey of a thousand miles begins with but a single step." Keep your eye on that single step, and the next, and then the next. The thousand miles will take care of itself.

By holding onto a winner, you can even do wonders for yourself! Everything I've described above can happen in your lifetime. As the price of your stock goes up, your net worth and your equity increases, so you can get credit for further investments.

Until I was halfway through middle age, I was shackled by a holdover tradition rooted in the depression. My parents, and thereby our whole family, developed an abhorrence of the use of credit. Hard times wiped out jobs and earning opportunity. Money was scarce. Survival meant managing on what you had. We bought only for cash and then only after intense comparison shopping. If you didn't have the money, you did without and waited until the cash was in your hands.

Whenever you bought on credit, you had to pay more. In those days, sources for installment shopping were limited, and you paid for the credit in more ways than just interest. The risk to the seller had to be factored into the price. Buying on credit also brought one a sense of boreboding, like a storm hanging overhead about to break at any moment. What if you couldn't pay on time? Your credit would be wiped out! What would you do in an emergency? The answer then was clear and emphatic: Only buy for cash!

For those of you who did not live through the depression, you can identify with this feeling if you've ever been overextended on your credit cards and wondered how in the world you would ever catch up. Perhaps you've sworn to yourself that if you could ever pay all this off, you would tear up the cards and never charge anything again!

The stories of the desperate calls for "more margin" in the crash of 1929, coupled with wipeouts and suicides, echoed and reinforced the admonitions of my parents: "Only buy for cash." Because of this background, I never had a "margin account." A margin account is a way of buying securities on credit by using your stock position as collateral.

Times change, however, and street smarts teach us to change with the times. As you build your portfolio of securities, mindful that you never sell unless you have a compelling reason, you will arrive at a point where you are fully invested—or at least as fully invested as you want to be. What happens, then, if you come across a company that seems just right, and its stock can be bought as a bargain?

First, you review your present holdings. Have there been any changes in the companies or the climate to warrant the sale of one of your darlings? If the answer is no, then the next step is to make a careful comparison evaluation between the proposed stock and each of your holdings. If the new stock is clearly superior to something in your portfolio, you have the elusive "compelling reason," and the stock can be sold to make room for the new one.

But what if it's a close call, and they all look good, and you are loath to sell anything? Then at last you take the dreaded step. You buy on margin—

BUT NEVER AT THE FULL LIMIT ALLOWED.

Leave a cushion of credit with which you can be comfortable.

If you find that being "on margin" makes you anxious, that's also a "compelling reason to sell." Sell some stock, pay off the margin of debt and relax.

Since everything in the market is a function of risk and reward, the theory is that the price of any stock at any given time in a free market is a reflection of balancing the relative risks and potential rewards involved. The same evaluation should be made of the risks and rewards of buying on margin. The less you borrow, the lower your risk of being caught short, that is, of being unable to "meet a margin call" and, as a consequence being sold out. The less you borrow, however, the less you have for further investment.

Now, if you're right and the stock you're acquiring and holding achieves greater growth, the collateral in your margin account will grow and support greater and greater credit (with only the same percentage of risk). As you continue to find sound growth companies, you can see important changes in your equity base within your own lifetime. The children and grandchildren need not be the only ones to enjoy your success.

There is another reason for having a margin account. The present securities regulations require that purchases be paid for in three business days. First the confirmation of the trade must be sent, then the check must be sent, so this regulation is used to avoid a "late payment." If you have money in your account—usually kept at the broker's in a money market account—the payment can be made on time. If your money market balance is too low, by having a margin account you can be advanced as much credit as the collateral in your account will afford to make timely payment.

Then, at your convenience, you can send a check (or sell off some stock to wipe out the margin balance owed).

Why send the check? Well, you do have to pay interest to the broker for the money advanced. And while the interest rate is competitive, it is surely more than you're earning in the bank. So it makes economic sense to reduce or pay off the margin. In addition, your account is then once again able to provide credit as needed.

Setting up your brokerage account as a margin account is like arranging with your bank for a line of credit on your checking account. If you should overdraw your checking account, the bank advances immediate credit to cover any checks that otherwise would have bounced. It reduces another source of anxiety and pressure.

CHAPTER TWENTY-SEVEN

Strategy Thirteen— Mutual Funds

Peter Lynch, the *wunderkind* manager of the Magellan Fund, in *Beating the Street*, says, "An amateur, who devotes a small amount of study to companies in one industry he or she knows something about, can outperform 95% of the paid experts."

This is a philosophy I strongly endorse.

The past twenty-five years have seen the awakening of the middle-class—especially the baby boomers. They finally realize that they must pay attention to their financial health and more important, do something about it! They discovered Wall Street and swarmed to get a piece of the action. During the same period we have witnessed the fantastic rise and expansion of mutual funds. These funds are investment vehicles whereby it is possible to buy an interest in a group of stocks selected by a professional who manages the buying and selling of securities in the fund for the fund's shareholders. In effect, the investor owns shares in the fund that owns the stock rather than owning individual stocks himself—rather like a co-op apartment. This gives the average person a chance to invest in the market without knowing too much about it, and without doing much work to find out. He is comforted by the belief that the money is being watched and grown by sophisticated professionals for the good of the fund's shareholders.

There are two major types of mutual funds: open-ended and closed-ended. In the open-ended funds, new shares are constantly being sold at a price determined by the pro rata value of each share at that time. It provides fresh capital for the managers to invest in the market. If you want to sell your shares, the fund itself buys them back by selling off some of its securities if there isn't enough cash on hand. The more people who invest in this type of fund, the bigger it becomes.

In a closed-end mutual fund there is a specific number of shares to be sold. Once they are all sold, you can buy shares only from another stockholder. The managers invest the original money raised, together with profits and dividends, and reinvest the money over and over again for the stockholders of the fund. With full disclosure of the securities held by the fund, the price becomes what a willing seller and buyer agree on—a free market determination. So in a closed-end fund, shares often sell at a discount or premium to the net asset value. Price depends on whether there are more sellers than buyers, or vice versa.

The mutual funds as originally set up provided a commission for those who raised the money. Typically, 8% of the money invested was taken off the top for the brokers and promoters who sold the mutual fund shares. As competition set in, the "load," or commission, was often reduced to 6% or 4% (in 1997 the average load was 4.3%). A new kind of fund—the no-load with no commission charged up front emerged. Regardless of how they advertise or set up, however, there are always rewards paid for raising the money. You never get something for nothing! A 1995 report for Goldman, Sachs & Co. on mutual funds indicated, "For all the talk of 'no load' and 'low load' investing, clients are paying more now than they were 10 years ago. Only now the fees are buried in distribution charges, fund expenses, contingent deferred sales charges, reinvested dividend charges, and so on."

I must admit that twenty-five years ago it occurred to me that creating and managing a mutual fund could be an interesting business. As a broker-dealer, I was privy to the phenomenon of mutual funds early on and was much impressed by their growth and popularity; however, after some thought and research, I concluded that although they were currently successful, there was no long-term future for mutual funds. In 1965 there was about $2.4 billion invested in the market through mutual funds. By 1997 mutual funds were over the $4 trillion mark and still growing! You can see I was a real financial visionary!

I was completely blind to the tremendous attraction mutual funds would have for middle-class America. Awake at last to the need to invest in the market for their financial future, millions of individuals since the mid-1970s have embraced the dream of having an expert, a professional investment manager, make investment decisions for them. Only the fabulously wealthy could afford professional investment managers before. The phenomonal growth of mutual funds is all so easy to understand in retrospect. Average middle-class investors knew they did not have the wealth or the knowledge or the background to swim in the shark-infested waters of Wall Street by themselves. And they did not have the confidence or choose to take the time to learn. So for a relatively small commission, they got a professional proxy to govern their investment. These were the same people who were paying 18% on their credit card balances every month, so a 6% commission didn't seem onerous!

In addition, the ferocious growth of mutual funds was promoted by the professionals—primarily because it was in the financial interest of thousands of Wall Street insiders to see it grow. Promoting mutual funds provides real money fast—now and perhaps for years. Let me explain.

When a broker convinces you to invest in the market, he makes a commission only when you make a trade. Once you've invested the money, there's no additional commission until you make another trade, that is, buy more or sell. If you're satisfied with your choices, nothing happens to create commissions for years. Unfortunately, the incentive for brokers to promote trades to generate a commission is not always in your best interest. This activity is called "churning." Often, that's how he earns his living.

Now, if your money is put into a mutual fund, there's a large commission earned immediately on the total money invested. Then there are annual management fees and transaction fees on a regular basis, and, of course, commissions every time a trade in the fund is made. Mutual funds are always churning the stocks and assets in their portfolios. They are wonderful for brokers and their firms.

Early in the history of mutual funds, the media promoted fund managers into familiar faces and created competition among the funds. Soon there were "stars"—fund managers as glamorous as anyone in Hollywood who achieved magical results. There were "manager of the year" contests and hijacking of "star talent" by one fund from another.

The financial media spotlight great performance reports each year to show the salivating public how easy it is to make money in the market. These reports create more and more believers and mutual fund stockholders. Of course, the funds that are featured are the big winners; mediocre, average, or losing funds are buried in the statistics. Every once in a while, a fund hits a home run, and the brokers and promoters make Wall Street ring with "hurrahs."

In 1995, a great year for the market generally, the

Bruce Fund grew an astounding 64.8%, just about double the gain on the Standard & Poor's 500 list of stocks. It is interesting to note, however, that the same fund averaged only 13.1% growth over a five-year return, lagging behind the 16.6% five-year run of the Standard & Poor's 500. By and large, over the years, mutual funds as a group have not done better than the S&P or Dow Jones averages; some have done better, and some have done much worse.

The funds have been fantastically well marketed. There are ads in every newspaper with a business section, every business magazine, on radio and TV financial programs. Seminars are offered by all the brokerage firms. Newsletters, pamphlets, and telephone solicitation are common. They haven't gotten to putting their faces on milk cartons yet, but watch out.

The fund manager probably does know more about Wall Street than you do at the start, but anyone who really wants to learn and has enough intelligence to profit from experience, personally and vicariously, can get a grip on the market. Nurture your own money. You don't need a nanny.

Successfully investing in the market is an exhilarating experience; it intensifies living. To be successful you must be involved with life—aware of everything that goes on around you. The market is affected by psychology, politics, foreign policy, science, medicine, new technologies, disasters, scandals, fads, and popular culture. The ability to recognize how events affect life is more important than the knowledge that the Dow Jones average rose or fell 6 points today.

As you become more sophisticated about how the market operates, you'll make more positive moves with your money: how much to put in equities, how much in bonds, how much in money market funds or CD's (cash), how much in large cap companies or small cap companies. How you deploy your capital will depend on your goals—what you want to achieve. Any change in your thinking can be quickly reflected in your portfolio. It is your investment package, and so it can be shaped to reflect whatever you want. Not so if it's all in a fund. The fund manager makes all the moves, and his goals are not always consistent with yours. Many of the funds are highly specialized—designed to invest in specific markets (e.g., growth, tax-free, international, bonds, utilities, science) and therefore limited to those markets.

The fund manager has the responsibility of running all the money in the fund, and his goal is to produce results that will keep the current fund holders and attract new ones. Hence, he has limited options; he can't take chances. It creates a kind of nervous management, with one eye on how other fund managers are doing and the other on the investments he has made. If he can do as well as the average manager, he probably won't get fired. Of course, your broker would have some of these same pressures if you relied only on his advice when you made an investment for yourself. But, normally, you control your broker.

On the other hand, if the fund manager wants to become a "star," he may become a gunslinger and take wild, impossible fliers with terrific odds in the hope that, if he hits, he will be number one that year, a financial superstar. This kind of action occasionally results in a phenomenally good year or two, followed by disastrous ones. Unfortunately, when he misses, it's your money, not his. The fund still gets its fees and commissions even when the manager was very wrong. The fund manager may have a very different agenda from yours—you're not necessarily following the same rainbows.

You may have surmised that I don't much like mutual funds. There is a place for some funds and for some people to be fund investors, but, generally, I see the funds somewhat like the camel that begged to get his frozen nose in the tent and then, bit by bit, moved deeper and deeper into the cozy atmosphere until he took over the whole tent. Funds are for the lazy.

In 1995 it was estimated that over 20% of all trades on the New York Stock Exchange were made by funds and that one-third of all American households had a mutual fund investment in one way or another. But that's not the real reason for my disdain. I am convinced that an intelligent man or woman with average education can individually, over time, do better than the funds. The funds are rooted in the erroneous belief that a manager can invest your money better than you can. Piffle. Remember the old Spanish proverb: "Under the master's eye, the horse grows fat." This is certainly true for Wall Street investors!

One other problem with mutual funds is that the types of stocks the funds invest in might not always sit well with your conscience. When you invest in individual companies, you can read their annual reports and find out if the companies you invest in share your ethics; you do not have that much control in many funds. Some funds will follow a particular ethical philosophy of types of investments; most do not. You might find yourself in a mutual fund investing in the very companies you dislike the most, including the one that downsized you out the door!

Here's another reason to have some misgivings about mutual funds: almost every mutual fund advertisement points up how fantastic the returns are for its stockholders. Invariably, the promoters find some unique aspect of performance to crow about, for instance, "best performance in the last 12 months" or "three-year average that beat the Dow." They know that performance sells mutual funds, and they feature it. Well, what do you do when there's no history of performance to shout about? When you have to start up a new fund, how do you attract the investor's dollars?

A coterie of mutual fund families have developed an

interesting gimmick to take care of that. It's known as "incu-
bation," and it has been applied one way or another by
many funds, including some of the household names like
Fidelity and the George Putnam Fund and Van Kampen.
It's a technique for selecting and testing new funds that will
attract the public investor. With a few hundred thousand
dollars invested by insider promoters, a baby mutual fund
can be started and operated in the twilight zone, away from
the attention of public investors. A special effort is needed
for the new baby fund to generate spectacular returns that
will catapult it to the ranks of top performance. Returns can
be unusually high because the operators are going for
broke. Normal weighing of risk versus reward is skewed
toward reward. Volatile stocks, new issues, and friendly traders can help get results. In addition, incubating funds often
do not allow redemptions by shareholders, thereby freeing
the funds from the problem of having cash or liquidity to
redeem. It's easy to see how such a carefully nurtured pre-
mature baby fund can achieve a stunning performance.

A mutual fund family may have a half dozen or more of
these "incubator" funds going at the same time, ostensibly
to perfect investment strategies. Limiting new investors to
its employees or citizens or its home state or simply not marketing the fund widely usually leaves it with less than $10
million in assets. Since the fund is registered, it is permitted
to use its performance record to encourage the general public to invest. That's how they're able to advertise "gain in
1996: 60%," with charts that look like the up side of Pike's
Peak! Needless to say, the operator picks the "preemie"
with the best record to attract the new investment dollars.

The savvy investor should cast a skeptical eye on newly
offered funds with fantastic performance records—somewhat like your reaction to an ad to lose weight without
dieting.

CHAPTER TWENTY-EIGHT

Strategy Fourteen— Managing Your Own Retirement Funds

You can usually do better if you manage your own money than if you rely on mutual funds. This is also true in other investment decisions you must make, like IRA rollovers, profit-sharing plans, and even when it comes to that sacred and vitally important account known as your pension plan. The knee-jerk reaction to the business philosophy of your pension plan is that it must be safe and conservative, built with rock-solid investments. The prime goal of professional pension plan managers is to keep the capital intact, not to grow the principal. Losing capital in a pension plan creates a blot on the manager's reputation that can never be eradicated. This philosophy is an absolute loser's game for the average pensioner.

If all you get is what you put in, with some incidental, conservative interest, you're not destined for a carefree old age. Sadly, almost the only thing you can be sure of is that the dollars you get back will be worth less than the dollars you put in. Unless you do something to cope with inflation, it will do you in! Even with our current low inflation, the value of the dollar continues to drop. Preservation of dollars should at best be a short-term goal. Over the long term, dollars shrink and fade, almost disappear.

Thus, when you're trying to plan for your old age, you must invest in ways to ensure that your assets will float with the rising tide. Equity stock in growth companies is your best solution to this problem. When the value of the dollar goes down, it will be reflected in the price of the shares. When you sell, you'll get more dollars back than you put into the stock.

Your pension fund can be geared to make a difference in your life when you manage it because you can decide what risks are worth taking and for what rewards. So much depends on where you are on the road of life. If you're just starting out, you can reasonably assume that you have a long way to go, and the investments you make in your pension plan or self-directed IRA should be selected for growth rather than for security. Even if you make some mistakes, you still will have many opportunities to catch up. Growth need not mean a crapshoot—it doesn't have to be double or nothing. Growth means investing in companies and industries that are expanding, that have pipelines to new products or services, that will have an important share of new markets.

The great advantage that IRAs and pension plans afford is freedom from taxes. No interest, dividend, or profit earned in an IRA or pension plan is taxed. The tax is levied when the money comes out of the plan, when you draw down your IRA or pension. In theory, you will be earning less then and therefore will pay taxes in a lower tax bracket. In the interim, IRA and pension money profits can be used for further investment and, it is hoped, greater profit and reinvested dividends.

This is truly a tremendous feature, as it gives you the advantage of compounding. Who has not seen the tables of bank advertisements highlighting the growing power of savings accounts through compound interest? Imagine the growth possible by compounding profits, dividends, and interest that equal or beat the index averages. This is not hard to do if you manage your own money. And you will enjoy it! I know scores of nonprofessional investors who have achieved great results without fanfare.

The greatest advantage of managing your own retirement funds is that you have no one to answer to but yourself. The professional manager is subject to review and must always account to someone else. He must be prepared to defend his every action and prove that his judgments were prudent. The pension fund managers in big companies have the added pressure of having to answer to their corporate bosses, whose personal wealth is tied up in the profit-sharing or pension plans of their companies. Imagine how conservative they have to be just to keep their jobs. (Your money is in the same pot with the big guys' money, but do you have the same objectives or the same constraints they do?) This has a powerful inhibiting effect on pension managers and results in super-safe moves that can never keep up with inflation.

To give you some idea of what a handicap a professional manager has, imagine that you are charged with taking care of your widowed mother-in-law's money. You know she's counting on it to support her for the rest of her life. Everyone in the family will know how you've done and likely express an opinion. Tough job!

Managing your own IRA or pension funds should be a breeze compared with managing someone else's. You can take some chances; you can assume the risks you're comfortable with and set the goals you want to achieve. And even if you make some mistakes along the way, you will have time and more experience on your side to get back on track. As you get older and closer to the day when your IRA or pension money will begin to come out, you may manage the investments differently. Once payout time is near, preservation of capital becomes important, perhaps more important than taking chances to increase it. Also the dread of inflation in the near future is not as debilitating. With inflation at 2 or 3% currently, your capital can be preserved with relatively safe interest returns. You can see that the management of IRA or pension money is a very personal affair and depends on your age and financial condition.

For married couples, both the husband and the wife should get involved. Their comfortable retirement concerns both of them, so both should plan the strategy for a growing retirement fund. Of course, they must each take some interest in the market and try to become as marketwise as possible. If one or the other turns out to have a great flair or interest in investing, there should be no problem if that person becomes captain. Or they may co-captain the investment ship and try to agree on every decision. Or they may divide the money and race to see who does better, only giving each other veto power on wild fliers. Couples will differ.

Some years ago my friend Howard, a young investment banker, became something of a legend on the Street with his string of exciting and successful new issues. His daring was a two-edged sword, however. He went broke a couple of times, but somehow always managed to come back. Then, while riding a crest, he pulled up stakes and moved out West. He had enough money to retire for life. But Howard could never sit on the sidelines. In a short time, he was deeply invested in his new state.

Visiting him in his new home, I was impressed with how quickly he and his wife had "gone native." He was dressed in boots, Levi's, and a cowboy shirt and kept a loaded gun in the trunk of his car. Their home was a colorful ranch. My first visit was a revelation: one can be happy almost anywhere. There was only one fly in Howard's ointment; I learned about it one quiet afternoon over a drink in his study.

Howard's wife, a lawyer, was a very bright woman. They had met in law school. She was privy to all his deals; they discussed every investment. The trouble was that when a deal or investment went sour, he never heard the end of it. She would bring it up again and again, pointing out all the flaws, the mistakes, the stupidity.

"You know," he told me, "I take chances, and sometimes I go wrong. But on the average I've done pretty well, and I don't mind losing once in a while. But she never lets up. The only thing she remembers are the losers. It's a pain."

"Well, Howard, I've got an idea for you. I know you tell her everything and she's your partner and advisor, but you really run the investment decisions. Why not make her a real player? Let her take some money, and see how she does on her own."

"What a great idea! I'll try it," Howard exclaimed.

Before I left he gave her a check and a short speech of confidence. I never heard another complaint from my friend about his wife. Maybe she was so good at the investment game that he was embarrassed to admit to me that now she ran most of the show and there were many fewer losers. Or maybe her percentage of hits was lower than his, and now she respected his judgment more. In any case, now they were true partners, and both were taking responsibility for their future. Both partners must become educated in the market, and both must learn to win and lose. But it's always nice to have your own little pot of gold, to take a few wild risks no one else needs to know about. Maybe the fruits of such labors will end up being a surprise world cruise for two, or just some money to blow for a weekend on the town!

CHAPTER TWENTY-NINE

Strategy Fifteen—Reading the Street for Mergers and Splits

Mark Twain has never been acclaimed for his financial know-how; if anything, he has been cited as an example of how a celebrity can dissipate his estate with bad investments. One of his books, however, which I read as an adolescent, provides insight into as to how and why so many people without specialized education have been successful on Wall Street. In *Life on the Mississippi*, Twain told of his training as a riverboat pilot who learned to "read the river." The gifted riverboat pilot learns to read the river. He knows what every swirl, streak of foam, jutting tree limb, or sudden widening of the river means and adjusts his course accordingly. These "river smarts" are not learned in school or from a book. Survival navigation results from close observation of changing conditions and intelligent interpretation of what they portend.

That's exactly what you need to make it on Wall Street—street smarts, like Twain's river smarts. You need to develop the ability to see things as they really are, rather than as what everyone says they are, the ability to recognize when the emperor has no clothes and the courage to act on your own conclusions. Above all, you must be attentive to the clues that beep out DANGER to the street smart and take appropriate cover. Reading the river is essentially geared to avoiding danger and trouble, like running aground or wrecking the boat; reading the street not only helps you avoid danger, it also opens up precious opportunities to make money.

Here are some examples of what I mean. In 1995 the banks had made a great comeback from their lows of 1993. The great majority were making money and were out of danger. But the impression even on the part of many professionals was that banks were still in trouble and therefore bad investments. Then there was great excitement generated by the fantastic pace of mergers and acquisitions and consolidations of banks into larger and larger conglomerates. The price paid, whether in cash or stock, was always at a premium over the trading price.

Ah, if one only knew which bank was going to be taken over, what a great chance to make a pretty profit. And the wonderful thing was that you didn't even have to wait until the takeover or merger actually happened (which often took months or even years). As soon as an announcement of a takeover or merger was made, the stock promptly jumped and traded higher, anticipating the future profit. So if you needed the money, or wanted to avoid the risks of the deal cratering before completion, you could sell at a profit, but at a somewhat lower price that reflected the risk still at hand.

The analysts and bank specialists feverishly search, check size, location of branches, share of the market, kinds and quality of loans, depositors, capital ratios, P/E ratios, cash flow, goodwill, book value, competitive edge, and a hundred other factors in each banking organization to see where and how they might fit. It is a monumental task, and the professionals, the MBAs, the merger and acquisition specialists are hard at work hunting for who is next.

But there's another way to pick up a clue that can lead to a big payoff. Mergers take months and months to negotiate, even after the principals realize there may be a fit and have started to talk. Secrecy is the order of the day; once the word is out, it plays havoc with the market, and the price of the stock can go into orbit and make the deal impossible to consummate. Needless to say, all the insiders are enjoined from buying or selling the stock. There's the clue! When an officer or director buys or sells the stock of his company, he must report the transaction to the SEC and to other agencies. This information is available to the public and is regularly reported by newspapers and financial services. This is invaluable information for the Street reader.

It has special relevance in our consideration of which bank may be next up for acquisition. In checking the insider activity of banks generally, you may note that one or more banks have had no insider trades for several months. Alert! That may very well be because the secrecy blanket has been cast, and there are negotiations under way. If you suspect a particular bank may be "in play" because it has no insider trades going on, and if a quick check of the vital statistics of that bank reveals that it might be a suitable candidate for a takeover, you have a big fat clue to act on.

Another example of reading the Street is the fairly widespread observance that stock splits result in an increase in the total price. This may be a self-fulfilling prophecy, because there is usually a surge in buying immediately after the announcement of a split in anticipation of the price rise. The split is effective because the price seems cheap to many, and also because the price is now at a level where more people can afford to own it. With stock of growth companies (particularly OTC companies), the price of the split stock often grows back to the original price within a year or so.

This stock split observation was refined by a very busy and successful doctor I met some years ago, who played the market as a hobby. Imagine my surprise when discussing the phenomenon of stock splits to hear how successful he had been in applying this knowledge. He looks especially for companies that have split in the past and then concentrates on prices that make the stock ripe for splitting again. He gave me the following examples:

Microsoft (MSFT)

Date	Price	Split
8/87	$128	2 for 1
3/90	$122	2 for 1
5/91	$117	3 for 2
6/92	$133	3 for 2
4/94	$130	2 for 1

Coca-Cola (COKE)

Date	Price	Split
4/86	$117	3 for 1
2/90	$76 3/4	2 for 1
2/92	$82 7/8	2 for 1

Here is another example, brought to my attention by a geologist who lives somewhere in the wilds of the northwestern United States. He has played the market with great satisfaction for the past twenty years. His favorite stock is the rather unglamorous Montana Power Public Utility. He was attracted to the company because of its vast holdings of natural resources rather that its electric power generation— and because of its regular high dividends.

In studying the company, he was intrigued by the relatively narrow volatility of the stock over the years. He reasoned that the great intrinsic value of its natural resources was a real buffer against a total collapse of the company, regardless of how interest rates might vary and in theory affect the profitability of the utility. He waited, and when the price looked as if it could be near the low for the year, he bought three thousand shares rather than the thousand shares of a stock he usually bought. He watched that stock and when it slowly worked its way up to 18% or 20% above what he paid, he sold. Mindful of the fact that he had also gotten handsome dividends along with his profits, he continued to monitor the stock closely. When last we spoke, he had traded that stock five times over the last six years with the same kinds of results. Reading the Street can sometimes be as specialized as one stock or a group of stocks—in this case the utilities.

Reading the Street is sometimes so obvious and so widely acted on that people overlook its importance as a strategy. The great long-term price moves start with changes—scientific breakthroughs that change the way we live, technological changes that affect our quality of life, new drugs, new cures, new kinds of entertainment, and so on. The great problem is how to recognize them. How do you assess the impact of the change or the cost of implementation or the time it will take? The same holds for the change that comes with disasters like hurricanes, earthquakes, fire, war, disease, and famine. The ripple effect comes into play here.

The changes that are dramatic and easiest to recognize are the consolidations or mergers of public companies and, conversely, the splitting of huge public corporations into two or more independent new corporations. The immediate market reaction is usually a surge in price, but then, as the excitement and glamour of the change wears off, the price settles down—for months and even sometimes for years. It's just another stock then. Nevertheless, as time rolls on, the stock reflects or validates the wisdom or folly of the original change in the price of the stock. Most of the time it is impressively up. For example, consider AT&T.

Possibly the monster split-up of all time in size and scope was the dismemberment of AT&T in 1983, following expensive years in court unsuccessfully fighting the federal government on monopoly charges. Seven "Baby Bells," as the regional companies were nicknamed, were created by spinning off shares in each regional Baby Bell to the former AT&T stockholders. Instantly, there were seven new public corporations with stockholders who knew very little about their new companies. Many of the new owners just couldn't be bothered with studying and assessing what they owned. After a quick rise in their profits, they dumped the stock in the new market for Baby Bells. Some thought of it as found money—a windfall. There were also new buyers anxious to get a share of the new public corporation at what they saw as bargain prices. Those smart stockholders who held on to the spinoff shares they received have been very richly rewarded, however. Not all seven of the Baby Bells did equally well, though. As with every other kind of stock, there is no substitute for doing your homework.

Mergers of complementary or even rival public corporations are easier to understand when you are reading the Street. First, there is the economy of size—the purchase of large quantities brings the unit price down. Second, overlapping jobs makes for a reduction in the number of employees, hence the reduced cost of doing business and improved profits. Third, managing money is easier. There are thousands of adjustments that will make for more efficiency.

The cost of getting to the new efficiencies however, can be staggering, for example, employee severance, capital write-downs, closing plants, selling discontinued operations at a loss, or adjusting prices. The reaction to the initial lowering of earnings can be devastating to the price of the stock. Sophisticated investors discount the importance of the early drop in earnings and hold on to the stock. They often recognize that this is an opportunity to accumulate a larger stake. Again, when the merger is first announced, there is great excitement and a move up in the stock price. Then as the results of operations trickle in, disappointment, loss of interest, and a sluggish performance. As the improvements and economies take hold, the earnings show the hoped-for growth; the price begins to take off, and the company becomes a winner.

Why should a spinoff or split-up be an opportunity to make money? A subsidiary or division becomes a new public corporation when the parent distributes shares of the subsidiary (tax free) to its stockholders on a pro rata basis. Sometimes it withholds a percentage of the new stock and becomes, in effect, the dominant or largest stockholder in the new company. Often a percentage is set aside to be sold to the public to raise fresh capital for the new entity, and then the balance of the shares are spun off to its stockholders.

The distinction between a "spinoff" and a "split" is one of size. Usually, a spinoff is a subsidiary or division engaged in a single activity, for example, exploration for oil (the Santa Fe Company) or a toy manufacturing (Fisher-Price).

A split, on the other hand, may be the separation of a large group of related enterprises of the major corporation. Each part may contain several operations or divisions. An example is the three-way split of ITT, which is creating three new, large, autonomous public corporations.

Following a spinoff or split, the new baby is tailored for success. The parent wants it to succeed; in essence, the shareholders of the parent are still the shareholders of the spinoff. Control is still in the same hands, so they give it every advantage they can: good management, a clean balance sheet, no long-term liabilities.

The new management team is given great incentives for success: options, profit sharing, pensions, higher job titles, and raises. They tackle the problem like entrepreneurs: they cut inefficiencies and waste and are innovative with new products and procedures. In a year or two, the spin-off blossoms into a very attractive company and is (history proves) three or four times more likely to be acquired or merged than the average public corporation.

This is no accident. The new company is usually a pure play; that is, its activity is in a single industry or operation. What you see is what you get. It is not fuzzied up with two or three different kinds of profit centers. It is easier for a competitor to buy, and it is also attractive to a company in a different field that would like to get a toehold in that specific industry or operation.

There's also a better climate for a deal. Remember, the controlling stockholders of the parent are usually still in control. They usually do not have the same interest or pride in the offshoot; they are more prone to take the money and move on. A sale or merger moves the price up.

After a few years, the new company should be judged on its own. Its history becomes irrelevant. The baby should be walking on its own—getting ready to run and jump— maybe to fly away to another large parent. Either way, stockholders who ride out the growing pains with the baby usually enjoy great rewards—long before the company reaches adolescence.

CHAPTER THIRTY

Strategy Sixteen—Find and Use Stockmates

There's another great advantage to investing in the market: it can be done very unobtrusively. If you want to be private about your success or failure, only you and your broker need to know. And if you have two or three brokers, even they won't know the whole story. There are so many people in the market buying and selling, investing and analyzing, that you're just another pebble on the beach. Being too secretive can cost you, however. The greatest learning experiences can come from other investors who may have been around longer than you and may be even smarter. Sharing information is the mother lode of opportunity.

But it's important to find the right people to share information with. They should be people who are willing to share with you, too, who believe you also have something to contribute. Below is a diagram that dramatizes the advantage of sharing knowledge.

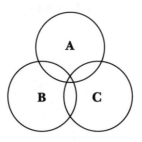

Each circle represents the total of knowledge and experience that an individual has vis-à-vis the knowledge of other individuals. As you can see, there is great overlap. In areas covered by A, B, and C, there is common knowledge—they all know that 2 + 2 = 4 or that February 14 is Valentine's Day, and so on. But there are some areas that only A and C have in common: they have both experienced and survived long hard winters, while B was brought up in Panama and never saw snow. B and C also share common knowledge: they were both orphans brought up by foster parents and know about Little League baseball. Both A and B speak Spanish and like salsa. The diagram makes it easy to see that some knowledge is shared by everyone, that other knowledge is shared by a few, and that each individual has certain knowledge and experience that is uniquely his or her own.

The remarkable thing about sharing knowledge is that there are only winners. For example, if you have a loaf of bread I want, you might sell it to me for $1. After the exchange I am a loaf of bread ahead (a winner) with a $1 loss (a loser). You are a dollar up and a loaf down. Both of us have come out "even." When you exchange information with a friend, you enrich each other at no cost to either of you.

What has this to do with investing? On Wall Street all decisions—what to buy, when to sell, when to double your position—involve information. The more facts you have, the easier it is to make the correct decisions. The thirst for information is insatiable. In advertising they say, "The more you tell, the more you sell." On the Street it's, "The more you know, the less you blow." Knowledge keeps you from making stupid mistakes; sharing ideas and information is key if the little guy is to make it. Look for that very special person or persons to share with as assiduously as you would search for the next Microsoft or Disney. Every time you find a "stockmate" to share with, you increase your chances for success.

Of course, you can have more than one stockmate. Monogamy is not necessarily a virtue on the Street. Your broker may seem like the perfect choice and in many ways may very well be, *but,* and this is a big "but," you have different goals. Remember, he makes his living from commissions and you do not. You pay him; he works for you. The relationship is not equal. Your community of interest is flawed.

There's another caveat: Be careful whom you select to be a stockmate. There are some people who are smart, who know their way around, and who consistently make money. These people are always good listeners when you have some special knowledge or insights to share, but, alas, they never share any special savvy with you.

Start out by assuming that anyone you'd like to share information with is a decent human being who will reciprocate. But don't give him too much rope. Be sensitive to the facts: if your stockmate only echos your own input, drop the leech. There are dozens of colleagues and business associates I share only closing prices with. They are sponges for OPI (other people's ideas/or information), but they never share ideas or information they think important. Often, they're the sort of people who believe that the only way to invest is with OPM (other people's money)!

Avoid OPM people because they think everyone but themselves is a sucker, and therefore is fair game to be taken. So no matter how attractive a deal looks, if the promoter or principal does not have his own money in it, pass. The passing parade of opportunities never ends for the ready mind. Just wait for the next bus.

CHAPTER THIRTY-ONE

Strategy Seventeen— Diversify with Bonds

I don't think very much of bonds for people who want to move up the financial ladder. Perhaps the reason is that I've never known anyone who became a quiet millionaire by investing in bonds. Many successful investors are heavily into bonds, but that's because for them they serve a different function. Bonds get to be important when you already have money and your primary goal is to hold on to it.

Bonds are a way of ensuring retention of capital and returns in the form of interest. There is less risk in bond investment when compared with equities. Ironically, there is also a world of difference in the degree of risk among the kinds of bonds offered. The safest bonds of all are the U.S. treasuries (T-bills), and therefore they yield the smallest interest. The amount of interest is also determined by the number of years the bond has until maturity: the longer the term, the longer the risk exposure, and the greater the interest.

Then there are municipals—bonds issued by states, counties, or cities—which sometimes have a tax advantage or tax-free feature. Each municipal bond varies in risk, length of time before maturity, etc. The lower the risk, the lower the interest, usually. But most municipal offer a better return than most T-bills. Triple tax-free municipals can give some taxpayers significant relief in cities like New York, where tax on income or regular interest is levied by the city, the state, and the IRS. Municipal bonds are also available through bond funds, not unlike mutual funds, except they are usually tax free—if the individual bonds in the fund would be if you bought them individually.

Various government agencies and similar institutional issuers, for example, the Federal Farm Credit Bank, the Tennessee Valley Authority, the Federal Home Loan Bank, and the GNMA Mortgage, offer bonds that are relatively low risk with relatively low interest. For those of you who like to support education, there are usually state-issued bonds for university systems like those in California and New York and in special university-building programs like UCONN 2000. These education bonds are tax free on your city or state income taxes, but may be subject to some federal taxes.

Corporate bonds are issued by public corporations (or utilities), and the rate of interest on each issue is determined by the strength of the corporation (or utility), the length of time before repayment, the price of money at the time the bond is issued, and the bond's optional recall provision. For example, the corporation may retain the right to pay off the bond before the due date if the cost of money (interest) drops enough. The corporation will "call the bond"—pay you off early and borrow elsewhere. Corporate bonds are issued for a period of years, but they can also be called earlier than the maturity date because the company is being sold, merged, or liquidated. In a liquidation, bondholders usually take precedence over other types of liabilities—except taxes and bank debt, which always come first. The market value of the bond varies, but the coupon (interest) never varies, as stock dividends may.

Whenever a treasury, municipal, or corporate bond is

offered, it has to compete in the market with the government, communities, or corporations that are trying to raise capital. The cardinal factor is the risk involved—a very tricky and difficult problem to solve. As a result, several bond-rating organizations have sprung up; Standard & Poor's and Moody's are the most prominent. They rate the bonds as to degree of risk in their judgment. Very often, their rating determines the amount of interest the bond will have to yield in order to raise the money. The highest rating calls for the lowest interest, the worst rating calls for a heavy price (interest) to compensate for the risk involved and to entice investors to take the gamble. The lowest risk is a bond with a AAA rating. Bonds with increasing risk are rated AA, A, AB, BBB, BB, C, and so forth.

Even after the bonds have been offered, sold, and distributed, the rating organizations review and assess the financial health of the company or municipality. As a consequence, the rating of the bond can change. A change in rating is closely noted by the financial community. The price at which the bond trades is affected by the new rating.

A serious drop in a corporation's bond rating is often an early warning signal that the corporation is in trouble. It is therefore important—even to the investor who is only interested in the stock—to keep an eye on the bond ratings. A low rating will make it harder and more costly for the corporation to borrow or raise money by selling stock. A drop in rating often precipitates sale of stock as well as bonds by cautious investors, thus driving the price of stock down and forcing any new stock issues to be sold at lower prices.

In short, bonds are safer than stock, but you can lose a great deal even when there is no bankruptcy or default! I learned this some years ago through the experience of my good friend Mark. He was an extremely engaging and charming young lawyer who switched careers when his brother-in-law became ill and needed help with his textile business. Mark's talent was put to good use, and the business grew beyond all expectations. When his brother-in-law passed away, Mark acquired his interest, and the business continued to grow. He built a beautiful home on Long Island, joined a very exclusive country club, and then sold the business to a famous conglomerate for what appeared to be a fabulous price at the time—$5 million—all cash!

When I asked him why he didn't take some stock in the conglomerate instead of cash and avoid some tax, he answered, "I'm not a pig—I'm happy to take the cash and pay the tax. When it's all done, I'm going to put a little over $3.5 million in thirty-year treasuries. With that sure 4% interest, I'll have over $150,000 per year for life. Remember, I never drew more than $100,000 in my best year. The house is all paid for. My kids are finished with school, and I'll never have a financial care again. Besides, they want me to run the business for the next three years with my old salary and bonuses. So why fool around and take a chance with stock instead of cash?"

The years that followed answered that question harshly. Inflation took off in the 1970s like a smallpox epidemic, and in the frantic efforts to control the runaway economy in the next few years, interest rates were raised again and again. New thirty-year U.S. treasuries hit an interest peak of 15%. Now the $150,000 per year that Mark got from his 4% could scarcely keep him in the lifestyle he was accustomed to. Yes, he did still have bonds in the face amount of $3.5 million. But unfortunately, when he attempted to sell some in the 1970s, he was crushed to find that the best he could get for a $1,000 face value thirty-year bond was about $350. Fortunately, the story has a happy ending. The conglomerate kept renewing his three-year employment contract and eventually sold the business back to him when it became clear to the corporation that only he could run it. They realized his constant threats to quit could be disastrous if he really did. Mark was a very smart businessman, but a lamb in the market.

CHAPTER THIRTY-TWO

Strategy Eighteen— Venture Capital

In managing your own money you are free to explore and make investments that a professional manager would never recommend or do. One of the most glamorous and risky kinds of investing is venture capital: very high risk investing, usually in start-up or new-research-based private companies. It means putting in money where the odds for failure are awesome but the potential returns can be fantastic.

The venture capitalist must be a visionary who can absorb the mumbo jumbo of the step beyond conventional science, technology, or medicine and see how the breakthrough being proposed will change the market if it becomes a reality. It is not enough to be right about the scientific step out; the venture capitalist must also make a correct assessment of the inventor or entrepreneur with the dream and his or her ability to get it to market.

Another investment hazard is who manages the money and how. It's sad how often the great idea, the new technology or discovery, is destroyed by inept management or the clash of egos.

Venture capital opportunities are not usually available for the individual with little capital. The SEC has rules establishing the minimum net worth of individuals who can invest in such deals, but the large amount of capital needed usually makes those rules academic. You can talk about it, think about it, but the reality is that few people can or should do it.

Nevertheless, one of the joys of managing your own money is that you can become a modest venture capitalist. You may not be on the cutting edge of science or discovery, but you may be a factor in the start of a new business. Investments do not have to be in megacorporations listed on the New York Stock Exchange or even smaller public corporations. Investments can be a small piece of a limited partnership, a part of your brother-in-law's new restaurant, or a real estate deal your accountant is organizing.

Sometimes the most meaningful and fruitful investments are those in which you are personally involved. It is these kinds of ventures that can lead you to a real change in your life. You can go from being a cog in the wheel to being the big wheel itself. Investments in small enterprises provide a window to the world of self-employment. You have a chance to see the details, why and how a business runs, and what an individual can do to make it successful.

Most professional venture capitalists have a position on the boards of the companies they invest in. They can ride management hard and become a real thorn in the side of sloppy management. The risks are so high that they demand and get a huge return on their investment when things go right. They hit only about one in five, but they make enough from the winners to finance their losses. Because of the huge risk, huge returns, and in-your-face involvement in the companies they capitalize, they are sometimes known in the Street as "vulture capitalists" or "gunslingers."

A very important rule in venture capital is never to invest more in a venture deal than you can afford to lose. Unlike holding stock in public companies, it's not easy to get out of a venture capital deal if the going gets rough. You can't find someone else to buy your stock when the company goes bad; you lose everything when it goes under. Legal entanglements often mar the experience and can make enemies of formerly good friends and relatives.

Part Three

Great Performances

In planning this book, I wondered whether research would support my preference for longtime holding. After selecting one hundred of the most successful public companies, I attempted to reach in person or by mail or telephone the chairman of the board, the president, or some knowledgeable corporate officer to answer two questions:

1. Why do you think your company has been successful?
2. How much would $1,000 invested in your company when you first went public be worth today?

The response was heartwarming, the help and cooperation generous. My questions required thought and even some courage to answer. Pinpointing and highlighting the underlying reasons for your corporate success poses a challenge of self-awareness and some candor.

The growth of the $1,000 originally invested, what with stock dividends, stock splits, mergers, spin-offs of subsidiaries, and reorganization, often required real digging into the financial history and metamorphosis of the corporation. In several cases, my contact just could not furnish the answer. The answers I did get were astounding, though!

What does this have to do with becoming a savvy investor? When a corporate executive candidly explains what accounts for the corporations' phenomenal success, there are clues to what to look for in other companies.

Three of the most recent winners are discussed in chapter 33. Ten more great performers are presented in alphabetical order in chapter 34. Finally, many more such companies are listed in the Appendix. The group gives you a lot of variety for study. Each is identified by a short description of its basic business and an exact quote or synthesis of the reasons my contact gave for success. Then I indicate the date the company went public or was reorganized so $1,000 could be invested, and its value in 1996 or 1997, when I interviewed each executive. The years between those dates vary considerably, so comparisons would be unfair and all but impossible. But one thing for sure—they all kept up with inflation!

Many of the companies are internationally famous, others are almost unknown and hidden from casual investors. There is a message here:

1. Just because a company is large and famous doesn't mean there is no more growth in its future. Many investors shy away from a company that has tripled or quadrupled in price. In the examples that follow, many have achieved prices 100 times or more the original offering price. Don't turn away too soon.

2. Unknown companies that have had fantastic success encourage you to look for tiny "acorns" everyone else ignores. Stick with your own judgment when everyone and his broker seem to pass on the company you like. Learn as much as you can about the company and, as long as it meets the criteria you've set up, stay with it!

CHAPTER THIRTY-THREE

Recent Winners: Amgen, Conseco, and Microsoft

In chapters 34 and 35, I present only a few of the companies that responded so generously to my requests for their secrets for success, not because these companies are more significant, but because I don't want to wear you out with dozens of examples once the advantages of long-term holding have been established. I've included the balance of the fascinating, inspiring, and thought-provoking companies in the Appendix. They should be studied for other reasons. Each of them may provide clues that will lead you to finding similar companies at an early stage of development, when your $1,000 investment will buy a bigger piece of the pie.

Get the current annual statement and also, if possible, a copy of the prospectus issued when the company last raised money. Scrutinize them both, as they contain a cornucopia of information to help you decide whether to invest. I cannot emphasize too strongly the need to ask "why" as you check. Be suspicious, suspect the worst, remember the influence of self-interest.

In all the corporations I discuss, success and growth continued long beyond usual expectations, and faithful stockholders were richly rewarded. A thread that ran through all the companies was a sense of pride in the company and its integrity. Again and again, the letters I received cited customer satisfaction and respect for people as employees or customers. Another recurring theme is the ability to change and adapt to solve customers' problems. Trusting and empowering employees to take risks paid off for many.

Ironically, there are several companies that have never left their original basic business. They have grown by expanding and reaching wider and wider markets. Others have changed so drastically that it's hard to unravel them to find what the original basic business was. Leapfrogging technology to meet the needs of the market was often the spur to their success and growth.

By and large, the companies avoided diluting shareholders' equity by declaring stock dividends and stock splits rather than cash dividends. In the main, they avoided heavy leveraging with borrowed money. Money was generally managed carefully and heavy interest payments avoided. Despite the longevity of the corporate existence, there were relatively few changes in corporate philosophy or style. The CEOs had long tenure and strong lines of succession.

Lest you become discouraged because you think from most of the thirty-eight examples that you will have to hold too long to be successful on Wall Street, here are some cheerful facts about corporations that made it straight away. Each of the three phenomenal companies I discuss in this chapter are in completely unrelated fields, but the success story is the same. How blessed is the loyal stockholder! There are so many ways to make it on Wall Street.

Amgen Company

Amgen Center
Thousand Oaks, CA 91320–1789
NASD symbol: AMGN
IPO: 1983

Amgen is one of the largest biotechnology companies in the world. Its great growth came from gene splicing and invention of two great products. Epogen is a red blood cell stimulator used to treat anemia in renal dialysis patients. Neopogen stimulates production of white blood cells, which fight infection. The company concentrates on cellular and molecular biology and soft tissue repair. Amgen has joint ventures with Roche, Johnson & Johnson, and Kivin.

Amgen was formed as Applied Molecular Genetics in 1980 by a group of venture capitalists and scientists to develop a few profitable products rather than to conduct general research. It first went public in 1983 with 2,350,000 shares at $18 per share. Splits of 2 for 1 in 1990, 3 for 1 in 1991, and 2 for 1 in 1995 reduced the cost basis for the original stock to $1.50 per share. With a share price in 1997 of approximately $62, an initial $1,000 investment in 1983 was worth about $79,000.

Conseco, Inc.

11825 N. Pennsylvania St.
PO Box 1911
Carmel, IN 46032
NYSE symbol: CNC
IPO: May 1987

Conseco, Inc., is a financial services holding company. Its life insurance subsidiaries develop, market, insure, and administer annuities and individual and supplemental health and life insurance products. Despite its conservative insurance approach, Conseco has acquired and restructured many insurance companies, as well as companies in riverboat gambling and racetrack operations. The company proudly proclaims that in the decade following its IPO in 1987, when over thirty-one hundred other companies went public, only five of them outperformed Conseco.

In May 1987, two million shares at $14.87 where sold to the public. After a series of splits, the adjusted cost basis for shares bought then is $93. In March 1997, with a price of $40 per share, the original $1,000 invested in Conseco was worth approximately $90,000. All this success with no exotic technology or scientific breakthroughs!

Microsoft Corporation

One Microsoft Way
Redmond, WA 98052–6399
NASD symbol: MSFT
IPO: March 1986

Microsoft was started in 1975 when William Gates, nineteen years old, dropped out of Harvard and teamed up with a high school friend, Paul Allen. They concentrated on computer software, and in 1980 were chosen by IBM to write software for the operating system for its new PC. This software (MS DOS) became an instant success and eventually a monopoly in the IBM-compatible world, as most other PC makers wanted operating systems compatible with IBM PCs for both home and office use. In March 1997, Microsoft's operating system operated approximately 80% of the PCs sold worldwide. Microsoft Corporation operates on the cutting edge of new technology and constantly introduces new products. It is now also an Internet challenger.

Microsoft's initial public offering was in March 1986, with 2.8 million shares offered at $21 per share. With split adjustment, there are now 100.62 million shares outstanding. The cost basis of shares bought in March 1986 is now $.58. The price as I wrote this in 1997 was over $100 per share. That means that $1,000 originally invested is now worth over $170,000. Not too shabby for a public corporation only twelve years old in 1997.

CHAPTER THIRTY-FOUR

Ten More Great Performers

After reading about the recent big hits like Microsoft, you may think that the companies described here and in the Appendix are a very select group—totally unrepresentative of reality. Of course, they are selective (I did the selecting), but my experience leads me to the conviction that there have been hundreds and hundreds of examples of listed and OTC companies where $1,000 invested at the right time would grow over one hundred times.

On September 30, 1996, the *Wall Street Journal,* in observance of the one-hundredth anniversary of the Dow Jones Average, reported that Ned David Research, Inc., had determined that $100 invested in the Dow Index, with dividends reinvested, would now be worth $61 million. This is a tremendous tribute to the powerful growth of compound annual investment in common stock over the long haul.

The following ten companies are presented in alphabetical order, because I am not making any value judgments or comparisons among them. There is enough variety in these thirty-eight great performers for you to find several that appeal to your particular interest. Find your own great performers and add to this list.

1. AFLAC Incorporated

132 Wynton Rd.
Columbus, GA 31999
NYSE symbol: AFL
IPO: 1955

AFLAC, Inc., is licensed in the United States and abroad to sell life, accident, health, and specialized insurance limited to reimbursement for medical and surgical expenses related to cancer treatment. It also owns and operates seven network-affiliated television stations in the southeastern United States.

Paul S. Amos, chairman of the board, has written: "My family started AFLAC in 1955 with just $40,000 in capital and some good ideas. Three years later we introduced the world's first cancer expense insurance policy. Today AFLAC has more than $24 billion in total assets."

He pointed out three tenets that made for this corporate success in the United States as well as Japan:

1. Always try to develop insurance products that fill specific customer needs at affordable prices.
2. Try to manage risk, not assume it. The business of insurance is assuming and managing risk, but in the investment of assets, keep risk to a minimum.
3. Take pride in providing quality service to customers, which is your best advertisement.

Kenneth S. Janke, Jr., senior vice president, advised me that $1,000 invested in 1955 would have bought ninety shares. Following twenty-six stock splits and stock dividends, the ninety shares would now be 42,614 shares and, at the end of April 1996, were worth $1.3 million.

2. Boeing Co.

7755 East Marginal Way So.
Seattle, WA 98108
NYSE symbol: BA
IPO: 1928/1934

Boeing Co. is a major producer of products for the aerospace and defense industries—commercial jets and military aircraft—and missiles for the U.S. and other governments internationally. It is one of America's top exporters, and has the world's most extensive network of field service bases and distribution centers. In 1997, it employed 105,000.

Paul S. Gifford, director, responded to my questions in a letter dated May 16, 1995:

> Question 1) This is a very difficult question because there is no single factor that has been the cause of our success. For the most part it is the result of our willingness to take risks and invest appropriately, the foresight to develop an entire family of products, and the ability and talents of our workforce. We have developed and maintained an excellent service and support capability for all of our products, both commercial and military, and we always try to listen to our customers.
>
> As was said in our 1995 Annual Report, "We have always prided ourselves on the quality, performance and reliability of Boeing products, but in recent years we've put a top priority on improving the progress by which we design, build and support those products. Our goal, in every product sector, is to be the value leader in our industry."
>
> Question 2) We first went public in 1928 as Boeing Airplane & Transport Company. On January 19, 1929, the name was changed to United Aircraft & Transport Corporation. Tracking the value of the stock issued at that time is very difficult because on May 14, 1934, the SEC forced a

reorganization, which resulted in the formation of three companies. One of those companies was Boeing Airplane Company, which later became The Boeing Company. The other two companies formed by the reorganization were 1) United Air Lines Transportation Corporation, which later became United Air Lines, and 2) United Aircraft Corporation, which included Pratt & Whitney, Chance Vought, Hamilton Standard, Northtrop, and Sikorsky. [Most of these companies are today part of United Technologies Corporation—Boeing's chief competitor.]

Tracking the value of the Boeing Airplane & Transport Company stock after the reorganization and through all the subsequent mergers and splits has not been possible at this time. However, if you bought stock in Boeing Airplane Company immediately after the reorganization in 1934, it would have cost you approximately $10 per share. For a $1,000 investment, you would have acquired 100 shares. Those 100 shares would have grown to 19,720 shares now, and would have been worth $1,619,500 as of April 1996.

3. Consolidated Papers, Inc.

PO Box 8050
Wisconsin Rapids, WI 54495–8050
NYSE symbol: CDP
IPO: circa 1911

Consolidated papers, Inc., produces and sells coated and specialty papers for the packaging and labeling of consumer products and food. It also manufactures display, container, and paperboard products. In 1997 it employed 5,931.

George W. Mead, chairman of the board, wrote me on April 15, 1996, that he said in a speech to stockholders on April 22 that the company's success was due in part to working very hard at being very good at what it does; as an excellent papermaker, the company has the know-how, the technology, and the market and customers. He told me:

> Your second question regarding the current value versus an original investment is really impossible for me to answer. We do have a corporate record showing some initial values dating back, believe it or not, to about 1910. Specifically regarding your question, there does not appear to be any time when we "went public." There were something like twenty original incorporators in 1894 or 1895, and the list of shareholders has expanded quite consistently ever since to its present total of some 7,000. Somewhere in the '40s we merged with another local firm, which has similar but not identical ownership, and I suspect that if I dug hard enough, I would find some stock issued at that point, but it would still not be an IPO.
>
> I can tell you this much: Going back to 1911 one share issued at that time would become 4,800 shares today due to stock splits and dividends over the years. Thus an investment in 1911 of five shares at $200 a share would become 24,000 shares today at $55 a share, or $1,320,000. How much of this is inflation? I suppose I could find out, but I haven't done so.

4. General Electric Co.

3135 Easton Turnpike
Fairfield, CT 06431
NYSE symbol: GE
IPO: 1892

General Electric Co. is a monster—appliances, broadcasting, communications, transportation, lightbulbs, satellites, jet engines, diagnostic imaging systems, diesel locomotives, etc. In 1997 it employed 222,000.

Joyce Hergehan, V.P. of corporate public relations,

wrote me on July 31, 1996, to advise that GE's chairman, Jack Welch, had been invited to ring the opening bell at the NYSE to commemorate the hundredth anniversary of the Dow Jones Industrial Average, since GE is the only original member on the Dow still in business. She continued:

> As you can imagine, there are many reasons behind GE's continuing success, but five that come to mind are:
>
> - Quality—The GE monogram is recognized as a symbol of quality throughout the world.
> - Technology—From its beginnings, GE has been a world leader in making technology work for people.
> - Creativity—GE is always looking for new ways to solve business problems or fill customer needs.
> - Leadership—GE is recognized worldwide for its management strength and leadership training.
> - Diversity of Businesses—Instead of being a single-product company, we have a mix of global businesses, from aircraft engines and appliances to broadcasting (NBC) and financial services, that are world leaders.
>
> A $,1000 investment in GE stock when we first went public in 1892 would be worth about $18,000,000 today, assuming reinvestment of dividends and based on a price of $85 per share in the second quarter of 1996. Over that 104-year period, we have had seven stock splits.

5. Hewlett-Packard Co.

3000 Hanover St.
Palo Alto, CA 94304
NYSE symbol: HWP
IPO: 1957

Hewlett-Packard Co. designs and manufacturers computers, calculators, work stations, video displays, printers, tape and disk drives, as well as medical diagnostic devices. Its products are marketed in the United States and throughout the world. Hewlett-Packard Co. has been one of the leading electronics companies for the last forty years and on the cutting edge of new products and applications.

Mary Anne Easley, manager of public relations services, advised me that $1,000 invested in HP stock in 1957 would have bought sixty-two shares. Through stock splits, each share in 1996 would have been 384 shares, for a total of 23,808 shares. Thus, in 1996 the original investment of $1,000 would have been worth $1,041,600.

6. Johnson & Johnson

One Johnson Plaza
New Brunswick, NJ 08933
NYSE symbol: JNJ
IPO: 1944

Johnson & Johnson is the leader in the fields of health care and pharmaceuticals. It caters directly to the consumer as well as to professionals. Its list of products includes a host of household names and products and nonprescription drugs, contraceptives, therapeutics, veterinary and dental products, surgical instruments, dressing and apparel.

While Robert V. Andrews, director of corporate communications, did not give me any clues for J&J's success, he did advise me that $1,000 invested in 1944, when the company first went public, was worth $1,538,060 at the end of 1995. In addition, the $1,000 investment would have brought $207,161 in dividends, for a grand total of $1,745,221.

7. Motorola, Inc.

1303 East Algonquin Rd.
Motorola Center
Schaumburg, IL 60196
NYSE symbol: MOT
IPO: 1954

Motorola, Inc., is a premier manufacturer of electronic equipment and components, with worldwide sales of paging and mobile communication devices, semiconductors, and special equipment for the military and the aerospace industry. In 1997 its employees numbered 142,000.

William J. Weisz, chairman of the board of this fantastically successful company, was kind enough to answer my inquiries:

> In response to your first question, we owe whatever level of success we have achieved to three fundamental points:
>
> 1) A belief in the necessity to deliver total customer satisfaction,
> 2) uncompromising integrity, honesty, and ethics, and
> 3) constant respect for people—the importance of the dignity of every individual. We believe that all else flows from these three points.
>
> You asked what a $1,000 investment in Motorola stock when the company went public would be worth today. . . . a $1,000 investment would have purchased 117.65 shares [in 1954], which in 1997 would be 74,542.14 shares. With a closing stock price of $65.75, these shares are now worth $4,901,080. This is an annual return of 17.40% for over 40 years.

8. Pfizer, Inc.

235 E. 42nd St.
New York, NY 10017
NYSE symbol: PFE
IPO: 1942

Pfizer, Inc., is a global research-based health care company that discovers and develops innovative medicines to meet the needs of patients and doctors.

Dr. James R. Gardner, vice president of investor relations, told me that Pfizer's success is due to focusing on its core competency—research—thereby discovering, developing, and marketing products that fulfill medical needs.

Pfizer spend $1.7 billion in 1996 on R&D. Bill Steane, the CEO, emphasizes sustained leadership through innovation. In 1995 Pfizer achieved its forty-sixth consecutive year of sales growth, twenty-eighth consecutive year of dividend growth, tenth consecutive year of top credit rating (Moody's and Standard & Poor's). It ranked 127 among U.S. companies in sales and 37 in net income in 1995.

Dr. Gardner told me that $1,000 invested in 1942, when Pfizer made its initial public offering of 240,000 shares at $24.75 per share—with seven splits since—would in 1996 have been worth 748 shares. In June 1996 Pfizer traded at $77³/₈ a share. The $1,000 would thus have been worth $2,025,949, and that does not include the dividends.

9. Regal-Beloit Corp.

200 State Street
Beloit, WI 53511–6254
ASE symbol: RBC
IPO: 1969

Regal-Beloit Corp. has two important lines of products: power transmission systems (i.e., gearboxes, hydraulic motors, and pump devices); and cutting tools for metal (i.e., taps, drills, reamers and saws). In 1997 it had 2,600 employees.

Robert C. Burress, V.P. and CEO, gave the following answers to my questions:

1) Stay focused in your business and do not wander too far out of those things you know, understand, and do best.

2) All top management is heavily involved in running our business. We know our customers and take an active part in staying close to all activities.

3) We watch and control costs, no matter how small, every single day. It is a part of our philosophy and a way of life for us.

4) Our plants are kept small (usually under 300 people) and are set up as profit centers. They are responsible for customer credit approval through customer payment and collections. This womb-to-tomb approach makes them much more responsive to specific customer needs. Our vice president/general managers at each of our plants are rewarded annually based upon their return earned on liquid assets, percentage of net income on sales, and true sales growth (volume).

5) Last, but certainly not least and probably most important, delivery to us is everything. We pride ourselves on getting product to customers faster than our competition and have done this since inception in 1955. Like watching costs, it is a way of life for us and we consistently do it better than anybody else.

In response to question 2, he wrote:

$1,000 invested in the Company when it went public in 1969 would have yielded an investment worth $27,000 today. Before the Company ever went public in 1969, we enacted several splits, otherwise appreciation would have been better. By contrast, for $500 invested when the Company was founded in 1955, that investment at the end of last year would have been worth $498,000.

This highlights the advantage of early investment—even before a company goes public. Hard to find, with much greater risks and rewards, but very early investments are the bread and butter of the venture capitalist.

10. Schering-Plough Corp.

One Giralda Farms
Madison, NJ 07940–1000
NYSE symbol: SGP
IPO: 1952

Schering-Plough Corp. markets an extensive line of pharmaceutical and consumer products, prescription drugs, over-the-counter medicines, vision care products, and animal health care products. Its brand names and trademarks are known worldwide. Its origins go back to Europe in the 1800s, and it was Americanized after World War II. Since 1971, when Schering merged with Plough, company revenues have grown, from $400 million to more than $5 billion in 1995.

Management believes that success has been achieved by maintaining financial strength, flexibility, and speed in adapting to markets and maintaining vigorous controls over costs. The company has also attracted and retained talented employees through rewards and challenges.

Although the answer to my $1,000 question was not readily available from the company, I believe that $1,000 invested in 1952 would have been worth $529,920 in 1996.

STREET TALK

The language of the Wall Street fraternity is unique and esoteric. New names and concepts are constantly being created to streamline, identify, and speed up communication.

To make life and the reading of this book easier, I have listed in the Definitions words that may be new or strange to you.

This street language is liberally sprinkled through the conversations of lawyers, accountants, brokers, security analysts, and your sophisticated friends. It is also used extensively in annual and interim reports, financial analyses, prospectuses, and financial literature concerned with the making of money.

DEFINITIONS

Accrued Interest Interest due under a bond to the time of settlement date. Bonds are traded "plus accrued interest" unless otherwise indicated.

Acquisition The purchase of a business of a public company for cash or stock.

ADR American Depository Receipts. Certificates traded like stock that are the evidence that a certain number of shares of a foreign corporation have been deposited to the owner's credit in a United States-connected bank abroad.

After Market Market activity after the initial offering and distribution.

All or None A special type of "best-efforts" underwriting in which the underwriter must sell all the securities offered or the deal is withdrawn.

Allotment The amount of securities set aside for a customer or a member of syndicate or a selling group.

Annual Meeting A meeting of stockholders held once a year to report on the affairs of a corporation, to elect directors who will manage the corporation for the ensuing year, and to vote on such matters that require stockholders' approval.

Annual Report Report issued by a public corporation once a year that gives the financial condition of the company, the president's message, highlights of the past year, and a statement by the company's auditors. Compare INTERIM REPORT.

Appreciation An increase in the value of an asset or security.

Arbitrage A technique used to take advantage of a price difference (usually temporary) in different markets or different forms of the same equity. For example, XYZ stock trades at $37^1/_2$ in New York City and at 38 in London—buy in New York and sell in London at the same time.

Asked   See BID AND ASKED.

Assets   Everything owned by a company. Compare CURRENT ASSETS.

At the Market   The price at which a security is currently trading.

Averages   Barometers of stock markets activity; you can measure or gauge what the market is doing. The Dow-Jones and Standard and Poor's are widely used and comprise listed securities.

Averaging   The purchase of stock at successively lower prices so that the average price for your stock is less than the initial purchase. Sometimes averaging is done on the up side as the price keeps moving up.

Baby Blue   Usually an OTC stock that looks as though it may someday develop into a blue chip.

Baby Bond   A bond that has a face value of $100 rather than $1,000.

Back Dooring   The practice of buying securities through one broker and selling them through another. Most frequent during a period of "hot new issues."

Back Office   The facet of the securities business concerned with the clerical, administrative, and paper-handling details.

Bailout   The sale of a block of securities by someone other than the corporation, usually one or more of the insiders. May be a partial bailout or total.

Balance Sheet   Shows in some detail the financial conditions of a company at some specific date, usually at the end of the company's fiscal year or one of the quarters.

Bear   Someone who thinks the market is going down. A bear market is a falling market. Compare BULL.

Bearer Bond   A bond that is not registered in anyone's name. May be transferred the same way as cash. The possessor is presumed to be the owner. Such bonds are No longer issued.

Best-Efforts   A type of underwriting in which the underwriter is only required to use his or her "best efforts" to sell the securities. In essence, he or she is acting as agent rather than principal for the company.

Bid and Asked   The bid is the highest price anyone will pay for a security at a particular time; the asked is the lowest price anyone will take at the same time. See QUOTATION.

Blue Chip   Usually a high-priced safe, solid, seasoned security, e.g., IBM.

Blue Sky   To comply with state laws concerning the public sale of securities.

Boilerplate   Standard legal language required by law or custom in prospectuses, debentures, corporation charters, etc.

Boiler Room   A high-pressure method of selling highly speculative securities, usually by telephone calls, telegrams, etc.

Bomb   A new issue that performs badly as soon as it starts to trade.

Boom   A period of active business, rising prices, widespread optimism, and speculation.

Break   A sudden and abrupt decline in price.

Bring Out   To offer a new issue of securities to the public.

Broad Tape   The Dow-Jones teletype machine that carries news likely to affect the stock market. It is called the broad tape to distinguish it from the ticker tape, which is narrow ($3/4$ of an inch).

Broken Lot   A number of securities less than the standard unit. In stocks, the standard unit is 100 shares; in bonds, $1000.

Bond   An obligation or debt of a corporation bearing a stated rate of interest and often secured by some of the company's assets and due on a specific date. A bond often has some provision for earlier redemption at the option of the company. The face amount is usually $1000, but published quotes are usually given minus the last digit (102¹/₄ means $1022.50).

Book Value   See NET WORTH.

Book Value per Share   The net worth of a company divided by the number of shares outstanding.

Broker   As applied to the securities industry, a person who acts as an agent for another (customer) in a securities transaction (compare DEALER); commonly used to indicate either the firm one trades with or the individual REGISTERED REPRESENTATIVE.

Bubble   An illusory or unsound business venture destined to evaporate when the bubble bursts.

Bucket Shop   A group of marginal, shady, unethical broker-dealers.

Bull   Someone who thinks the market is going up. A bull market is a rising market. Compare BEAR.

Business Cycle   The theory that there is a recurring cycle composed of prosperity, recession, depression, and recovery.

Buy In   When a seller fails to complete a contract, the buyer may buy the security in the open market, after proper notice to the seller, and charge the loss, if any, to the seller.

Call   An option to buy a particular stock at a set price for a specific period of time. Compare PUT. See also STRADDLE.

Capital Gain   Profit made on the sale of capital assets such as real property or securities. Short-term gains of one year or less are taxed at regular rates. Long-term gains are taxed at lower rates.

Capital Loss   Loss derived from the sale of capital assets such as securities or real estate. Up to $1,000 of such loss may be deducted from taxable income for the year reported. If the loss is more than $1,000 then $1,000 of it may be deducted each year for five successive years.

Capital Stock All classes of shares that represent total ownership of a corporation.

Carrying Charges Interest charged by a broker for carrying customers' securities on margin.

Cash Flow The amount of cash generated by a company during a specific period. This may be more significant than the stated earnings in assessing the value of a business and may also be very important in forecasting the company's ability to pay its debts.

Cats and Dogs Highly speculative low-priced stocks.

Certificate The actual price of paper that serves as evidence of stock ownership in a corporation.

Chartist A person who makes or interprets charts on graph paper showing the activity of a particular stock.

Churning The practice of buying and selling securities for the prime objective of creating commissions; the practice is unethical and against regulations.

Close, The The period at the end of a trading session; the final trades for a particular day.

Close Corporation A privately held corporation.

Closely Held Corporation A large percentage of corporation stock is in a few hands and held for long-term investment.

Commingling Mixing customers' securities with those of the broker or other securities for the purpose of collateral, etc.

Commodity A movable article of commerce such as wheat, corn, cotton, pork bellies, or coffee.

Common Stock Shares of a corporation that usually carry voting rights and that may receive dividends resulting from earnings.

Confirmation Notice sent by a broker to confirm a transaction in securities. It contains all the basic terms: trade date, amount, price, tax, settlement date, etc.

Conversion Price   The price used to compute the number of shares a company will give in exchange for its convertible bond or preferred stock.

Convertible Bond   A bond that gives its owner the right to exchange it for a specific number of shares of stock.

Correction   Price reaction to an excessive swing up or down.

Coupon Bond   Coupons representing the interest due and attached to the bond; they are cut off and presented for payment at the appropriate time.

Cross   A securities trade in which a broker represents both the buyer and the seller.

Curb Exchange   The American Exchange.

Current Assets   Those assets that can be readily turned into cash.

Current Liabilities   Obligations due within one year, i.e., taxes, accounts payable, interest, and loans.

Cyclical Stocks   Stocks that move with the business cycle.

Dealer   A firm or person who deals in securities transactions as a principal. Almost all securities firms are authorized to act as broker-dealers, so they may be acting in the capacity of agent or principal. They are required to indicate the capacity in which they are acting on the confirmation slip.

Debentures or *Debenture Bonds*   Bonds without any specific collateral or security for the debt.

Depletion   The allowance for the replacement of assets being used up—oil, copper, gold, etc.

Depreciation   A special fund to replace assets that are wearing out—furniture, fixtures, machinery. A certain percentage of the cost is set aside each year so that when new equipment is needed the money will be there.

Dip   A mild setback in price.

Directors   The persons elected by stockholders to manage and direct the affairs of the corporation.

Disclosure The requirement that all pertinent facts be disclosed to the public, e.g., that broker-dealers indicate on confirmation slip whether they were acting as agent or principal.

Discretionary Accounts Those accounts in which the broker is given the authority to buy and sell for the customer.

Dividend That share of a corporation's profits that the board of directors has voted be paid to stockholders for each share of stock they own. It may be distributed as cash, additional stock, or even property.

Due Diligence The investigation and examination that must be made by an underwriter to determine the worthiness of a corporation to be underwritten.

Dump To unload stock in a hurry.

Earnings per Share The net profit divided by the number of shares outstanding.

Effective Date Date on which a security has been cleared by the SEC for sale.

Equity Value, after all claims and liens are accounted for.

Escrow The placing of something for safekeeping with an impartial agent.

Evening Up Taking a profit to offset a loss, or vice versa.

Ex-dividend The buyer of a stock selling ex-dividend does not receive the recently declared dividend. This is important in checking quotes or recording prices, usually expressed as XD.

Execution The completion of a buy or sell order.

Expiration Date Day on which rights, options, or other privileges expire.

Fail Any security not delivered or received by the contractual settlement date (five business days after the trade date).

Fall Out of Bed A sudden or sharp drop in price for no apparent reason.

Fiduciary   One who acts in a position of trust and confidence concerning money matters.

Fill or Kill   An order to complete a buy or sell order immediately or it expires.

Finder's Fee   Brokerage fee paid for bringing parties together, as mergers or underwriting.

Firm Bid   A bid that is good for a certain period of time.

Firm Undertaking   When an underwriter agrees to buy securities from a corporation at a fixed price whether he or she can resell them the public or not.

"Flat"   Used to describe bonds or other indebtedness traded without interest added on.

Float   The number of shares in the hands of the public and available trading.

Flurries   Sudden, short-lived price movements.

Free Credit Balances   Funds held by the broker that a customer has an unrestricted right to withdraw on demand.

Free Riding   The practice of buying new issues and selling the securities before they have been paid for; also the allotment of "hot" issues to family and business associates.

General Partner   One who shares the profits and is personally liable for the debts of the partnership.

Gilt-edged Securities   High-quality bonds; the term probably originated in the days when bond certificates had gold edges.

Goodwill   An intangible asset that enhances the earning power of a company, i.e., reputation, connections, location, management, efficiency.

Gross National Product   Total market value of all goods and services in the nation; an index or gauge of the nation's business activity reported periodically by the U.S. Department of Commerce.

GTC   "Good till canceled" order; this order remains in effect until either executed or canceled. Compare OPEN ORDER.

Heavy Market   One that tends to go lower, i.e., that has more sellers than buyers.

Hedging   An action taken to protect loss in another operation. Example: buying convertible bonds to protect short sale of the stock. If the price goes up, the bonds may be converted into stock to cover the short sale.

Hidden Assets   Assets that do not appear in the corporation reports but are nevertheless real assets to be taken into consideration when evaluating the corporation.

High-Grade Stock or Bond   One that enjoys the highest investment rating.

Hit the Bid   Sell to the highest bid at once, before it can be changed.

Holder of Record   The name appearing on the transfer books of the corporation as the owner as of a certain date.

Holding Company   A corporation that owns all or the majority of the stock of one or more other corporations; usually not an operating corporation.

Hot Issue   A new issue for which there is great demand; usually opens trading at a premium.

Hot Money   Capital shifted from country to country in search of higher interest rates or quick profits.

House Account   An account maintained by a brokerage firm for its own trading or investing.

Hypothecation   The pledging of customers' securities as collateral for loans by brokers and dealers; the written permission of the customer is needed.

Inactive Stock   A stock that is traded infrequently.

Indicated Market   The price at which a broker believes a security may be bought or sold when there is no firm market.

Indication   An expression of interest in buying proposed securities that have not yet been cleared for sale.

Insider Reports   A requirement by the Security and Exchange Commission that all officers, directors, and owners of more than 10% of a company whose stock is listed on a national exchange and also certain over-the-counter companies must report all purchases and sales made by them of the company's stock and the number of shares owned directly or indirectly at the end of each month.

Insiders   Those who hold unregistered stock of the corporation and are in positions of management and control.

Institutional Investors   Institutions whose operation requires a high level of investment—banks, pension funds, churches, hospitals, etc.

Interest   Money paid for the use of capital.

Interim Report   A report issued by a corporation other than its annual report. Compare ANNUAL REPORT.

In the Black   To operate at a profit.

In the Red   To operate at a loss.

Investment   The placing of capital in real estate, securities, or business in which the risk is relatively low for the purpose of gain through income or profit.

Investment Banker   Similar to an underwriter except that he or she often invests in new industries or young companies for his or her account.

Investment Club   An informal group of people who invest jointly in selected securities.

Investment Letter   A letter containing a representation that the securities being purchased are for investment only and not for resale.

Investment Trust   A company that uses its capital to invest in other companies. There are two principal types: the closed end, in which the number of shares remains fixed, i.e., in the hands of a stockholder who already owns shares and is willing to sell; and the open end or mutual fund, in which the number of shares is not fixed and in which the company issues more shares as people want them. It also may buy back its stock in relation to its net asset value at the time of purchase.

Involuntary Investor   A trader or speculator who can't sell because he or she has a loss.

Issue   Securities, i.e., stocks, bonds, debentures, etc.

Issue Price   Price at which new issues are first offered to the public.

Issuer   A corporation that issues its stock for sale and distribution to the public.

Joint Tenants   Co-owners of a security; both signatures are needed to transfer. When "with right to survivor" are added, the securities automatically belong to the survivor on the death of one of the joint tenants.

Joint Venture   An enterprise launched by two or more principals for their joint benefit.

Kill   Cancel.

Killing   A very large profit.

Kiting   Pushing stock prices to unwarranted high levels.

Lamb   One who is inexperienced in the ways of Wall Street and follows the flock blindly.

Late Tape   When trading is so heavy that the ticker can't keep up with transactions.

Layoff   When a broker who has agreed to purchase securities under certain conditions makes arrangements with other brokers to sell part or all of the securities involved.

Lead Indicator   A statistic concerned with some facet of the economy that analysts believe gives a clue to what the future will be for the economy as a whole.

Letter or *Lettered Stock*   Stock that has not been registered with the Securities and Exchange Commission and cannot be traded publicly. The buyer signs a letter that states that the stock is being purchased for investment. The letter may also contain a proviso that the stock will not be sold for a specific period of time.

Letter of Comment   A letter from the SEC itemizing questions to be answered and corrections to be made in a prospectus. Compare RED HERRING.

Letter of Intent   An agreement between the underwriter and the corporation relative to the proposed sale of securities and setting forth the essentials of the deal.

Leverage   Application of the principle of the lever to finance; the movements of large amounts of money (both up and down) by the skillful application of small investment. Examples: (1) buying stock on margin; (2) high debt structure for corporations; and (3) buying warrants.

Liabilities   Everything a company owes. See CURRENT LIABILITIES.

Limited Order   An order to buy or sell a security at a specific price. It may also be limited as to time, with the order expiring if it is not filled by a certain time or date.

Liquidity   Ease with which assets may be turned into cash.

Listed Securities   Those traded on a national stock exchange such as the New York Stock Exchange and the American Stock Exchange.

Load Charge   The commission charged the buyer of most mutual funds.

Locked In   A condition under which the investor can't sell his or her securities because of taxes or agreement or security regulations.

Locked Up   Withdrawn from circulation, as when securities are placed in strong and conservative hands for long-term investment.

Lockups   Companies that will be liquidated with the expectation that the liquidation value per share will be higher than the current market price per share.

Long   A customer or broker is "long" (holding) those securities he owns. Compare SHORT.

Lot   A unit of trading.

Majority Stockholders   Those who own controlling interest in a corporation.

Make a Market   A dealer who buys and sells regularly and stands behind his bid-and-asked prices is said to make a market in a particular security.

Margin   The practice of borrowing money in order to buy securities that in turn are used as collateral for the loan. Margin may also mean the amount or percentage of money borrowed.

Margin Call   A request for additional cash or collateral to bring equity up to the percentage required by law or a broker's good judgment.

Market Letter   The price at which stock is traded in the open market.

Maturity   The date on which a bond or loan becomes due and payable.

Member Firm   A broker-dealer that is a member of a national exchange, usually the New York Stock Exchange or the American Stock Exchange.

Merger   The joining of two or more public or private companies with an exchange of securities rather than cash; usually only one corporation survives.

Minority Stockholder   One who owns less than 50% of the outstanding shares and does not control the corporation.

Miss the Market   To let an opportunity to buy or sell profitably slip by.

Municipals   Bonds issued by cities, towns, states, housing authorities, and other government agencies responsible for maintaining such public facilities as schools, highways, and bridges. Interest on municipal bonds is usually free of some taxes and often free of all taxes.

Mutual Fund   See INVESTMENT TRUST.

NASD   National Association of Securities Dealers, Inc.

Net   That which is left after all deductions.

Net Profit   Usually the last line on the profit-and-loss statement to show how much money the company made during the period indicated.

Net Subject to Call   Bonds that cannot be paid off before maturity date.

Net Worth   The difference between all assets and all liabilities; also known as book value.

New Issue   A security being offered to the public for the first time by a corporation that is going public.

None Offered   A condition under which no one is offering to sell the stock.

NOTC   National Over-the-Counter Clearance Corporation.

NSTA   National Security Traders Association, Inc.

Odd Lot   Less than a round lot. See ROUND LOT.

Off   Lower prices: "The market is off."

Offering Circular   A special type of prospectus used for 504 underwritings—i.e., those under $1,000,000.

Offer Wanted   An invitation by someone who wants to buy.

Officers   The people usually elected by the board of directors to run the corporation on a day-to-day basis.

Off the Board   A transaction made over the counter and involving a listed security.

Offering Price   The price at which a security trades once it has been cleared for trading by the SEC.

Open Order   An order limited as to price but unlimited as to time. Compare GTC.

Option   The right to buy shares of the corporation at a specific price prior to a set date. Options are usually granted only to individuals and may only be exercised by them or their estates.

Option Writer   One who supplies stock option contracts to put-and-call brokers for resale to the public.

OTC Market   Over the counter market. The market that handles all the securities business in the country not transacted on registered exchanges. Many securities traded on registered exchanges are also traded over the counter.

Outsiders   The general public.

Outstanding Shares   The number of shares issued by the corporation and held by stockholders.

Out the Window   Used to describe a new issue so easily sold that the distribution was as effortless as throwing the stock "out the window."

Overbought   A market that is too high.

Oversold   A market that is too low.

Oversubscribed   When orders for new issues exceed the supply.

Paid in Surplus   The amount of money paid to the company in excess of the stated par value of the stock. See PAR VALUE.

Painting the Tape   Causing a stock to appear often on the tape to give the illusion of great activity; a form of illegal manipulation.

Panic   A severe financial collapse, usually of short duration.

Paper Profit   Profit that has not yet been realized on a security.

Parent Company   A company that owns or controls another company.

Par Value   The arbitrarily designated value of a stock set by corporate charter.

Pass a Dividend   When a corporation does not declare a dividend at a regular expected time.

Penny Stocks   Low-priced stocks, sometimes under $1. The term is often used to describe any over-the-counter stock under $10.

Pink Sheets   At one time, stack of legal-sized pink sheets containing daily quotes on approximately eight thousand company securities (also twenty-five hundred bond quotes on similar yellow paper). Today pink sheets are weekly, not daily.

Pit   The trading floor for commodities.

Place   To find a market for a stock.

Plunger   One who speculates in a big way.

Point   Unit of market price fluctuations. In stocks, a point is $1; in bonds, it is $10.

Portfolio   The holdings of securities by an individual or institution. A portfolio may contain bonds, preferred stocks, and common stocks of various types of enterprises.

Position   An inventory of securities.

Preferred Stock   Stock on which there is some preference over common stock usually with regard to dividends, which may be at a fixed rate. Preferred stock may have preference over common stock in the distribution of assets in the event of a liquidation. Preferred stock may or may not carry the right to vote for directors.

Premium   The difference between the original offering price and the price at which a stock trades at the opening.

Pretax Earnings   Earnings before deductions for taxes.

Price Range   The highest and lowest prices reached by a security during a specific period.

Primary Distribution   When first-time securities are publicly offered for sale.

Prime Rate   The rate of interest charged by a bank to its best borrowers.

Priority   The order of rights. Important in the liquidation of a corporation, as it determines the order in which creditors and security holders are paid off.

Private Placement   Money raised by sources other than a public offering.

Profit-and-Loss Statement   A rather detailed list of the company's income and expenses for a stated period of time.

Profit Taking   Turning paper profits into real profits by selling.

Proxy Fight   Where two or more groups struggle for control of a corporation and seek to get the proxies (votes) of the common stockholders.

Put   The right to sell shares of a particular stock at a set price for a specified period of time. Compare CALL. See also STRADDLE.

Quick Assets   Cash or liquid assets that are quickly convertible into cash, e.g., U.S. notes or obligations.

Quorum   The minimum number necessary in order to conduct business, for instance, at a board of directors' meeting or annual or special stockholders meeting.

Quotation   The price at which a trader stands ready to either buy a specific security or the price at which he or she is prepared to sell that security at a given time. Commonly known as a "quote." See BID AND ASKED.

Rally   Price recovery of an individual stock or the general market.

Rate   Percentage of interest.

Reaction   The temporary reversal of an upward price trend, usually caused by some unfavorable news.

Read the Tape   Follow price changes on the ticker tape.

Realize   Sell a security and take the profits.

Recapitalization   A form of reorganization that changes in some way the capital structure of the corporation.

Receiver   One who is appointed by the court to take charge and run a business until it is reorganized or liquidated.

Recession   The downward phase of the business cycle.

Record Date   The date fixed to determine the owners or holders of securities as of that date.

Recovery   A rally in the market following a decline.

Red Herring   A prospectus describing securities that has been filed with the SEC but not yet released so that securities can be sold to the public (name derived from cautionary language printed in red ink). Compare LETTER OF COMMENT.

Refunding   Replacing an issue of securities about to fall due with a new issue.

Registered Bond   A bond issued in the name of the owner.

Registered Representative   An employee of a securities brokerage form who is registered with an exchange or the NASD as having passed prescribed tests and met certain requirements. He or she is authorized to serve customers of the firm in securities dealings.

Registration   The process of obtaining clearance from the SEC to sell securities to the public.

Regular Way Delivery   Delivery by selling broker to buying broker on the third full business day after sale. With government bonds, regular way means next-day delivery.

Regulation "T"   A Federal Reserve System regulation that pertains to the extension and maintenance of credit on securities.

Regulation "U"   A federal regulation governing the amount of credit advanced by banks.

Reorganization   The financial reconstruction of a corporation.

Report   The verbal confirmation of purchase or sale at the time of transaction.

Reserves   Funds set aside periodically for a specific purpose.

Resistance Level   The price level for particular stock or financial index at which selling pressure has been stepped up on more than one occasion.

Reverse Split A reduction in the number of outstanding shares. A 1-for-4 reverse split would reduce 2 million outstanding shares to 500,000.

Retained Surplus An item reflected on a balance sheet to indicate money earned by the company that has not been paid out in dividends.

Rigging The illegal practice of artificially keeping or forcing prices up.

Rights Similar to warrants, except that they usually have a much shorter life.

Ring A group of individuals working together to either raise or lower the price of a security.

Risk Capital Speculative funds employed in a venture of considerable risk.

Round Lot A standard unit of trading, usually 100 shares for stock. Sometimes in high-priced securities, the round lot is 10.

Runoff The last trades as printed on the ticket after the close.

Salt Down Stock To buy stock and prepare to hold it for a long time.

Saturation Point When the supply of stock exceeds the demand.

Scalpers Fast traders who work on small profits.

Seasoned Stocks The stock of well-established companies.

Seat on the Exchange Membership in a national exchange. The New York Stock Exchange, founded in 1792, is the largest.

SEC The Securities and Exchange Commission, established by Congress to supervise and regulate public corporations and their securities.

Secondary The sale of securities by someone other than the corporation itself.

Selling Group Broker-dealers who sell part or all of a public offering as agents rather than as underwriters who act as principals and assume more responsibility.

Selling-Off   Declining prices.

Sellout   What occurs when buyer fails to accept delivery in accordance with the terms of a contract. The seller may without notice "sell out" all or any part of the securities for the best available price and hold the buyer liable for the loss, if any. Also the sale of enough securities to cover a margin call.

Session   A period of trading activity.

Settlement Date   The day on which a buyer must pay for securities bought and the seller must deliver certificates for securities sold.

Shade   A small decline.

Shell   A public corporation that has few or no assets or business and is not active.

Shoestring Trading   Operating on thin margin.

Short   Customers or brokers are "short" when they have sold securities they do not own. They must deliver these securities at a later date (by purchasing or borrowing). Compare LONG.

Short Selling   The practice of selling stock you do not own in expectation of buying the stock later at a lower price. In the interim, the stock must be borrowed so you can deliver on your sale.

Short Term   Less than one year.

Signature Guaranteed   The practice whereby a brokerage firm or bank guarantees the signature of the registered owner of a security.

Size of Market   The number of shared bid for and the number offered at the prices quoted. Example: 3 and 1 would mean that the bid is good for 300 shares and 100 shares could be bought at the offer price.

Sleeper   A stock whose price is quiet but that is nevertheless attractive for strong potential gains.

Small Business Investment Company (SBIC)   A company licensed and regulated by the Small Business Administration and designed to provide capital to small business. Long-term loans from the government at low interest rates and special tax considerations provide the incentive for operating this type of business.

Soft   The tendency of a stock to seek lower price levels.

Soft Money   Business or commissions in exchange for research or service.

Solvent   Used to describe a corporation or individual when resources are available to pay all debts as they become due.

Specialist   The member of the exchange who has the responsibility to maintain a fair and orderly market in the stock or stocks he or she services. A specialist matches buyers and sellers and also buys and sells for his or her own account to stabilize the market.

Specialist's Book   The book composed of orders to buy and sell at prices other than current market price. There is a separate book for each stock.

Spin Off   Distributing or apportioning all or part of a subsidiary corporation's stock on a pro rata basis to the stockholders of the parent corporation.

Sponsorship   Support of a particular stock by one or more interested parties.

Spread   The difference between the bid and asked prices; also the difference between the price the underwriter pays for stock and the price at which it is sold to the public.

Spurt   A short, sharp advance in price.

Stabilize   To keep prices from fluctuating or changing radically.

Stamp Taxes   Required by many states on security transactions; stamps are paid for by the seller.

STANY   Security Traders Association of New York, Inc.

STAQ   Security Traders Automated Quotation System.

Start-up Costs   Costs involved in putting a new plant or business into operation for the first time.

Steady   Used to describe firm market prices, with little fluctuation.

Stiffened   Used to describe firming tendencies toward higher market prices.

Stock Dividend   When stockholders receive stock as a dividend instead of cash; this type of dividend is usually tax-free and enables the company to retain cash for working purposes.

Stockholders   Those who own shares or stock in a public or private corporation.

Stock Jobbing   The business of creating, manipulating and unloading stock on the public.

Stock Power   An assignment form used to make the transfer of securities easier.

Stock Split   When more shares are created by splitting the number outstanding. In a 2-for-1 split, stockholders get an additional share for each share they hold.

Stop Order   An order to sell stock at a specific price or to buy at a specific price.

Straddle   A combination put and call for the same stock for a specific period of time. See CALL; PUT.

Street   Wall Street, i.e., the securities market.

Street Name   When the owner of securities leaves them in the name of a broker; this makes for ease of transfer and availability for use as a collateral.

Supply Area   The price level at which a stock will be offered for sale.

Support the Market   To enter buy orders at a specific price in order to stabilize.

Suspend Trading   To prohibit trading in a stock for an indefinite period.

Suspension   The prohibition of a broker's privileges for a stated period.

Swing   Price movement up or down.

Switching   The selling of one security and the purchase of another for some advantage.

Syndicate   A group of investment bankers or brokers who form a formal group to underwrite and distribute a new issue of securities or a large block of an outstanding issue.

Take a Bath   To take a large loss.

Take a Flier   To take a big chance for a possible big gain.

Take a Position   To buy a block of stock in expectation of a rise or to sell a block short expecting a fall in price.

Tape   A mechanical device that prints the volumes and prices of security transactions within minutes after the trades.

Tax Exempts   Bonds issued by states, cities, or their agencies; the interest on these bonds is partly or fully exempt from federal income tax and may also be partly or fully exempt from state income tax.

Tax Selling   Selling securities to establish a loss that can be used to offset a gain and thus reduce tax liability.

Technician   A chartist or individual whose market forecasts are derived from study of the technical fluctuations and position of the stock involved.

Tender Offer   An invitation for stockholders to tender their securities for sale under the terms set forth; may be made by the corporation itself, another corporation or an individual.

Thin Market   Used to describe a small number of shares available for trading; may result in wide swings both up and down.

Third Market   Transactions in listed securities by over-the-counter brokers rather than through a national exchange.

Tie-in Sales   An illegal agreement between underwriter and customer under which the customer will buy a certain number of shares of a new issue in the after market if he or she is allotted some shares at the offering price.

Tight Money   When interest rates are high and credit's tight.

Timing   The art of deciding when to buy or sell.

Tip   Inside information, concerning a stock.

Tombstone   An advertisement in a newspaper or magazine describing securities released for sale; the language and information are so limited by laws and regulations that it appears like information on a tombstone.

Top Out   To level market prices after a long upward move.

Trade Date   The date on which a trade took place.

Trader   A person who buys and sells securities for his or her firm's account in the act of maintaining a market or who buys and sells securities as an agent for a customer. A trader is required to state in which capacity he or she is acting on the confirmation sent for each transaction.

Transfer Sheets   The transfer record of changes in ownership of securities as issued and maintained by the transfer agent.

Treasuries   U.S. government negotiable bonds; these differ from E, H and other government savings bonds in that these "treasuries" or "governments" are marketable and may fluctuate in price; savings bonds are price-fixed and cannot be traded.

Treasury Stock   Stock issued by a corporation that is later reacquired, usually by purchase.

Trend   A price movement in a given direction.

Turnaround   A situation in which corporate or business problems have been solved and it is believed or hoped that the company will turn around.

Turned Over   Sold.

$2 Broker   A member of a national exchange who specialized in acting as a broker for other brokers on the floor of the exchange. The name describes the fee that was once paid for each order executed. They now operate on a sliding scale.

Undertone   The basic condition of the market, strong or weak.

Underwrite   To undertake the sale and distribution of securities for resale to other brokers, institutions, or individuals.

Underwriter   A firm or individual who undertakes the sale and distribution of securities to the public.

Unissued Stock   The difference between authorized stock and stock already issued.

United of Delivery   Stock: 100-share certificates; bonds: $50 or $1,000 face-amount.

Unload   To dump or sell.

Venture Capital   Risk capital.

Volume   The number of shares traded during a given period.

Voting Right   The right of a stockholder to vote on the election of directors or other corporate matters.

Voting Trust   An agreement to permit trustees to vote stock in trustee custody.

Warrants   Rights to buy shares at a specific price for a definite period of time; usually assignable and frequently traded like stock.

Wash Sale   Buy and sell orders by the same persons within a short period to give the illusion of great activity.

Watering Stock   The technique of overstating assets of a corporation and thus increasing the apparent value of the stock.

When Issued   Used to describe a security authorized but not actually issued.

Wildcat   A highly speculative venture.

Window Dressing   The practice of arranging the affairs of a company to create a more-favorable impression.

Wire House   A broker-dealer who is associated with other broker-dealers by means of private wires.

Withholding   The illegal practice of selling or allotting more than normal amounts of securities in a hot new issue to financial associates or members of the immediate family or the underwriter of the selling group.

Working Capital   Current assets less current liabilities.

Write Off   To cancel a debt or claim.

Yield   The ratio of annual dividend to current price. A $3 dividend on a stock selling at $100 would have a 3 percent yield.

Yo-Yo   A stock that moves up and down like a yo-yo.

More Great Performers

1. Albertson's, Inc.

250 Parkcenter Blvd.
Boise, ID 83726
NYSE symbol: ABS
IPO: 1959

Albertson's, Inc., is the sixth-largest retail food and drug company in the United States. Started in 1939, its earnings grew from $10,000 that year to $162.5 million in 1989, with sales of over $6.8 billion in the latter. By 1988, one store had grown to 725 supermarkets and combination food and drugstores, primarily in the West, with a recent entry into Florida.

Joseph A. Albertson, founder, built the chain on the philosophy: "Provide the widest range of products at the lowest possible prices, and give the customers lots of tender loving care." There were over 80,000 employees in 1997.

A $1,000 investment in 1959 would have been worth over $100,000 in 1996, and over $11,000 would have been received in dividends.

2. Amp, Inc.

470 Friendship Rd.
PO Box 3608
Harrisburg, PA 17105–3608
NYSE symbol: AMP
IPO: 1956

Amp, Inc., is a world-famous producer of electronic and electrical connections, program, and switching devices, terminals, connecters, and data entry systems. It has 175 manufacturing facilities in twenty-eight countries and in 1997 employed 40,800.

Selwyn Friedlander, director of corporate staff services, advised me that $1,000 invested in 1956 at $16.25 per share would have been 6,912 shares worth $297,000 in May 1996—without dividends.

The history and philosophy of the company is reflected in a book published to commemorate its fiftieth year: *The Amp Story: Right Connection.* It gives fulsome credit to its inventor, management, and loyal employees. Success has come from constant adaptation and change.

3. Archer Daniels Midland Co.

4666 Faxies Parkway
PO Box 1470
Decatur, IL 62525
NYSE symbol: ADM

Archer Daniels Midland is one of the largest food processors in the world. It buys and sells agricultural products, processes oilseeds, corn, wheat, peanuts, rice, flour, and cane sugar. It stores, refines, and transports worldwide.

Dwayne O. Anderson, the prominent chairman of the board, was kind enough to answer my questions as follows:

1. Our company is midwestern oriented among a large pool of the best businessmen in the world: farmers. A great deal of our executive personnel has been drawn from farm-oriented, farm-educated agricultural schools.
2. Approximately $120,000 would be the value of the $1,000 invested since they went public.

4. Cooper Tire and Rubber Co.

701 Lima Ave.
Findlay, OH 45840
NYSE symbol: CTB
IPO: 1960

Cooper Tire and Rubber Co. manufactures automobile and truck tires, inner tubes, and vibration controls, such as hose and tubing, auto sealing, and sealing parts. Its products are sold through independent dealers and distributors. It employed 8,284 in 1997. The company furnished the following answers on May 17, 1996:

1) Why do we think Cooper has been so successful? Back in 1926, a customer and benefactor to Cooper was a man named I. J. Cooper. He had a business creed that we have adopted, and have "updated" over time, but it is still the same basic three ideas:

Good merchandise
Fair Play
Square Deal

We have included a little write-up about the creed, but the key to making any program work is the people. We have outstanding, motivated people who have a common focus—

our customers. We want to be the best supplier our customers have ever had. I might point out that we have received a number of service awards each year from customers who have a supplier rating program.

2) Cooper was first listed on the New York Stock Exchange on July 11, 1960. Our stock symbol is CTB. Caterpillar Tractor already had CT, so we added "B" for Mr. Brewer, who was then President and Chairman. On July 11, 1960, the average trade was $15.06, $1000 would have purchased 66.4 shares. Since that time our shares have split a number of times. These original 66.4 shares have grown to 3,187 shares. At a price of $24.00 per share, the initial investment has grown to $67,488.

5. Eaton Corp.

Eaton Center
Cleveland, OH 44114
NYSE symbol: ETN
IPO: 1923

Eaton Corp. manufactures products for the transportation, construction, and aerospace markets worldwide: truck transmissions and axles, engine components, hydraulic products, electric power control equipment, and ion implanters. It employed 52,000 in 1997.

Stephen R. Harris, chairman of the board and CEO, generously took the time and effort to answer as follows:

> We began in 1911 with an innovative truck axle and parlayed that into a dynamic business, serving truck and passenger car markets. We grew with these industries and succeeded because we met or exceeded the expectations of our customers. We've always been prudently managed and had dedicated employees. That's a potent combination: great products, a focus on the customer, excellent management, and dedicated employees.

At Eaton, we spent the 1980s squeezing excess and inefficiencies out of our manufacturing processes, pushing quality and productivity up and costs down.

In 1982 for example, we were concerned that Japan might enter the heavy truck transmission business—one of our core strengths. We began exploring how microprocessor control could enhance transmissions. As a result, today we are not only a low-cost producer, but we are also launching electronically enhanced automated transmissions.

To sum it up, Eaton's management has been nimble. They have reacted to change and learned to adapt quickly. In recent years, we have become even better at this skill. We have enlarged our vision, and we're constantly finding new ways to help our customer's success, finding new technologies to enhance our products and capitalizing on new market opportunities.

With regard to your second question, $1000 invested in Eaton in 1923 would be worth approximately $79,000 in 1996.

Mr. Harris's answer points up the need for heads-up management to handle competition. Bet on people rather than on products.

6. Ecolab, Inc.

Ecolab Center
370 Waleosha St. N.
St. Paul, MN 55102
NYSE symbol: ECL
IPO: 1957

Ecolab, Inc., develops specialized cleansing, sanitizing, and maintenance products and services for farm and dairy. It also provides institutional pest control, janitorial, and "Klenzade" products in worldwide markets, particularly

Canada, Latin America, and the Asian pacific. Its employees numbered 9,000 in 1997.

Michael E. Shannon, chairman of the board and CEO, wrote in June 1996 in response to my inquiries:

> We believe Ecolab's success is the result of ultimately one key element—an aggressive focus on solving customer problems with cost effective, value-added product and service solutions.
>
> From the earliest days of our company, the Ecolab culture has been to do whatever it takes to help our customers. To accomplish this, we have developed the industry's largest and best trained sales and service force. Our people partner with our customers to fully understand their problems and develop effective solutions to their needs, and to do so on a worldwide basis. This has proven to be a sound—and lucrative—growth strategy for our company.
>
> In answer to your second question, $1,000 invested in 1957, the year our company went public, would be worth $142,000 today—a 14% compound average growth rate.

No need for microchips, Internet, high tech here. The road to riches often comes from the mundane, the everyday needs of the average person.

7. General Dynamics Corp.

3190 Fairview Park Dr.
Falls Church, VA 22042
NYSE symbol: GD
IPO: 1952

General Dynamics designs and builds nuclear submarines for the U.S. Navy and tanks for the Army and Marine Corps. It also offers repair, engineering, and support services. Shares were first issued in 1952, and $1,000 would have purchased 32 shares then. After several splits, they would have grown into 968 shares worth about $61,000 in 1996.

W. Ray Lewis, staff vice president added that the success story for the current management team began on January 1, 1991, when $1,000 invested would have bought 40 shares. With splits and dividends reinvested in General Dynamics stock, the $1,000 would have been worth $10,000 in 1996—a truly remarkable achievement for a mature company in the last six years.

8. Genuine Parts Co.

2999 Circle 75 Parkway
Atlanta, GA 30339
NYSE symbol: GPC
IPO: 1948

Genuine Parts Co. is a wholesale distributor of replacement automobile and industrial parts as well as office products. It operates sixty-four NAPA warehouse distribution centers in the United States. Products include industrial bearings, power transmissions, material handling equipment, agricultural and irrigating equipment, and office furniture. In 1997 it employed 23,000.

Larry Prince, chairman of the board answered my questions on May 30, 1996, and modestly claimed that the company's success could be attributed to being in a sound industry. The company has continued to market replacement parts in three basic and necessary markets and has not taken forays into unfamiliar areas. It has had only three CEOs since its founding in 1928. With a highly decentralized approach to management, the corporate headquarters group, with fewer than 200 people, manages revenue of

$5.2 billion. "At GPC we believe we have to find a way to improve our results every month and especially every year compared to the previous period."

A $1,000 investment in 1948 would have bought ninety shares at $11 per share. After nine stock splits, it would have been worth over $600,000 in 1996, exclusive of $200,000 in dividends paid through the years.

9. Hartford Steam Boiler Inspection and Insurance Co.

One State Street
PO Box 5024
Hartford, CT 06102–5024
NYSE symbol: HSB
IPO: 1866

Hartford Steam Boiler insures boilers and energy equipment. It supplies engineering services and inspection to ensure code compliance for nuclear power plants and other power plants. Hartford Steam Boiler's mission is as relevant today as it was in 1866: "To benefit businesses, government, and industries worldwide by providing services and consulting, in risk management, safety, reliability, and efficiency."

R. Kevin Price, senior vice president, wrote in 1996 that the company's strategic focus was to help customers avoid losses rather than paying insurance claims for them: "We use our technical expertise to help our customers."

As for the $1,000 investment when the company went public, he writes: "Based on paid-in capital of $500,000 in 1866, the year the firm went public, and the current market capitalization of approximately $1 billion, the original $1,000 investment would be worth approximately $2 million.

10. Hasbro, Inc.

PO Box 1059
1027 Newport Ave.
Pawtucket, RI 02862–1059
ASE symbol: HAS
IPO: 1968

Hasbro, Inc. is a worldwide leader in the design, manufacture, and marketing of toys, games, interactive software, puzzles, and infant care products. Its trade names and brands include Playskool, Kenner, Tonka, Milton Bradley, Parker Brothers, Hasbro Interactive, Mr. Potato Head, Tinker Toy, G.I. Joe, Batman, Scrabble, and Monopoly. Hasbro has built an international franchise for children's products.

Wayne S. Charness, V.P. of corporate communication, advised me on May 20, 1996:

> There are many reasons why Hasbro has become the successful company that it is. We have the absolute best library of brands and products in the world and we continue to grow them. Our operational philosophy revolves around:
>
> 1. Building our core global brands,
> 2. Broadening our product base, and
> 3. Taking opportunities as we search out new areas to grow.
>
> We are proud of our management team and our employees, who help us do what we do best—bring smiles to the faces of children.
>
> According to our calculations, $1,000 worth of stock purchased when the company went public in 1968 would be worth approximately $73,000 today.

11. H. J. Heinz Co.

600 Grant Court
Pittsburgh, PA 15219
NYSE symbol: HNZ
IPO: 1946

H. J. Heinz manufactures and distributes food products such as ketchup, sauces, pickles, tuna, pet food, vinegar, and frozen potatoes. Weight Watchers International, a subsidiary, operates and franchises weight-loss centers and licenses diet foods worldwide. In 1997 the company employed 42,000.

Debora S. Foster, general manager of corporate communications, advised me in 1996 that H. J. Heinz Company was marking its fiftieth year on the NYSE. It first appeared there on October 15, 1946, with an initial offering price of $41. One hundred shares purchased then would have been worth $1,511,147 in 1996. To keep our analysis consistent, $1,000 invested in 1946 would have been worth $377,787 in May 1996.

12. Illinois Tool Works

3600 West Lake Ave.
Glenview, IL 60025
NYSE symbol: ITW
IPO: 1961

Illinois Tool Works manufactures products for the aerospace, appliance, automotive, truck, electronics, and computer markets, plastic and metal fasteners, testing equipment, adhesives and coating systems, and industrial packaging. W. James Farrell, chairman of the board and CEO, answered my questions as follows:

1) Why do I think our company has been so successful?
—A focus on decentralized companies with management and people given the latitude to be assertive and the trust to take the risks.

2) How much $1,000 invested when the firm went public is worth today?

In 1961, $1000 invested would be worth $200,000 today.

Another example of a nonglamorous business that gets glamorous results.

13. Keystone Industrial, Inc.

9600 West Gulf Bank Drive
PO Box 40010
Houston, TX 77240
NYSE symbol: KII
IPO: 1965

Keystone Industrial, Inc., manufactures industrial valves for controlling liquids, gases, and solid materials. Sales and service are available worldwide to the food and beverage, water and sewage, natural gas, petroleum production and refining, pulp and paper, and power industries.

Mark E. Baldwin, V.P. and chief financial officer, advised me in 1996 that Keystone's success came from bringing new technology to the market and developing new markets for that technology. The second reason was a surge of business in Europe, the Far East, and Latin America.

A $1,000 investment in 1965, with dividends reinvested, was worth $147,791 in 1996—for a compound annual growth rate of 18.12%.

Being "firstest with the mostest" can be a powerful reason for success, particularly when coupled with good management and drive. Keep your eye open for companies designing technological improvements, even though they are not very glamorous.

14. Lee Enterprises, Inc.

130 E. Second St.
Davenport, IA 52801
NYSE symbol: LEE
IPO: 1969

Lee Enterprises, Inc., is in the communications business. It owns a chain of nineteen daily newspapers, six television stations, and many weekly magazines, primarily in the Midwest. In 1990 it celebrated its hundredth anniversary—a testament to the six leaders who built the company and set the tradition of family for all employees. At the time the company employed 5,600.

Lloyd G. Schermer, chairman of the board and past president, wrote me on May 2, 1996:

> I was shocked and pleasantly surprised to learn we had done so well at Lee. I guess that's part of my answer to your question. My focus was always on operations and results. The stock price seemed to take care of itself. I never did the sort of tally you sent in your letter. We always followed the most conservative accounting practices and put the highest priority on being candid and honest with shareholders, employees, and customers.
>
> When I read about "downsizing" I wonder where those managers have been all of these years? If you grow an organization, it should always be lean. My highest priority was to attract, motivate, and retain talented people. They make it all happen for the stockholders. My job as CEO was to choose the course, keep the company on that course, and

maintain a balance between the best interest of the share-holders, employees, and customers.

I also tried to keep my ego under control. I wasn't spending shareholder money but my own. That's how I felt. Size is not the measure of success. What you do for each shareholder is what counts.

Charley Munger and Warren Buffet were attracted to Lee when I became CEO back in 1973. Charley's company bought 11% of Lee and he has been a very close friend all of these years.

A $1,000 investment in 1946 yielded fifty-one shares in 1960, when Lee Enterprises was formed. It has grown in value to $223,000 on November 15, 1988. Lee Enterprises did not go public until 1969, when it traded over the counter. A $1,000 investment then was worth over $50,000 in 1996.

15. Leggett & Platt, Inc.

One Leggett Road
Cuotbage, MO 64836
NYSE symbol: LEG
IPO: 1967

Leggett & Platt, Inc., is a leader in manufacturing engi-neered furniture and bedding products for the home, of-fice, and industry, for example, box springs, tops, coils, lumber frames, spring wires, cotton cushioning for beds, au-tomobile seats, etc.

J. Richard Calhoon, V.P. and assistant treasurer, advised me in 1996 that, under the leadership of Harry Cornell, Jr., who became president and CEO in 1960, there had been concentrated focus on management's commitment to achieving identified goals and objectives in niche markets.

On April 24, 1996, $1,000 invested in 1967 would have

been worth $112,500, exclusive of dividends and fractional shares, indicating an annual return of 17.8% over a 29-year span.

Even the most humdrum business can be a gold mine. Unglamorous, basic manufacturing can produce a glamorous bottom line. Look for the sleepers.

16. Leucadia National Corp.

315 Park Ave. So.
New York, NY 10010
NYSE symbol: LUK
Reorganization date: 1978

Leucadia National Corp. is a financial services holding company principally in personal and commercial insurance and banking, lending and manufacturing. The company has concentrated on investment and cash flow rather than on volume or market share.

Shareholders' equity grew from a deficit of $7,657,000 on December 31, 1978, to positive equity of $1,111,491,000 on December 31, 1995. Control of the company passed to the company's present chairman and president in 1978.

In the 1995 annual statement, the chairman, Ian M. Cumming, and President Joseph S. Steinberg give a remarkably candid explanation of their strategy and method of operation, including an admission of very poor performance in manufacturing. I particularly recommend reading and studying this report, since the price of this stock in 1978 at $.08 a share (adjusted for stock splits) was trading as high as $40 a share in 1998. A $1,000 investment in 1978 would have been worth $480,000 in 1998.

This is obviously a corporation led by two highly gifted entrepreneurs. The caveat for shareholders must be, "Who will be there for the encores?"

17. Lowe's Companies

PO Box 1111
North Wilkesboro, NC 28656–0001
NYSE symbol: LOW
IPO: 1961

Lowe's Companies is a "do-it-yourselfer" with a vengeance. It has 365 stores in twenty-three southern states. It sells building materials; lumber; hardware; appliances, kitchen, bath, and laundry products; yard and garden tools; and heating and cooling systems. Robert L. Strickland, chairman of the board, wrote in May 1996:

> We strongly believe that our success is rooted in two fundamental principles:
> *Keeping tabs on what our customers want and need from us and responding aggressively to those needs with products, prices, and services that meet or exceed their expectations.
> *Employee ownership—Lowe's is an ESOP company with between 15% and 20% of the company's stock controlled by current and retired employees. Over time, our employees have witnessed first hand how their commitment to the growth and success of the company is rewarded with growth and success in their personal fortunes.
> As a result, $1,000 invested in our company when it went public in 1961 would have purchased 82 shares of stock. Through splits and stock dividends, that number would have grown to approximately 9795 shares, with a market value of roughly $343,000, for an average annual growth rate of 18%.

In addition, the company is taking a greater and greater interest in television programs geared to the do-it-yourself market. The annual statement is a joy to read.

18. Nucor Corp.

2100 Rexford Rd.
Charlotte, NC 28211
NYSE symbol: NUE
IPO: 1973

Nucor Corp. manufactures steel and steel products, including hot-rolled and cold-finished steel shapes, joists, girders, wide flange beams, steel disk and grinding balls. Distribution is to the steel service renters—manufacturers and general contractors. F. Kenneth Iverson, chairman of the board, answered my questions in April 1996:

It is difficult to write a short answer to your question of why Nucor has been successful, but some of the factors are:

1. Lean management.
2. Strong concerns for employees and utilization of incentive systems.
3. Pushing decisions to the lowest level (Corporate office only 23 people).
4. Avoid legal costs.
5. Avoid debt (will not leverage Company more than 30% debt to total capital).
6. Encourage innovation.
7. We have stayed in our core business—manufacturing and steel products.

Based on the information he furnished, $1,000 invested in 1973 would have been worth over $140,000 in 1996. This is another example of how a rather prosaic and competitive business can achieve spectacular results.

19. Pepsico, Inc.

700 Anderson Hill Rd.
Purchase, NY 10577–1444
NYSE symbol: PEP
IPO: 1965

Pepsico, Inc., operates a worldwide business in soft drinks, snack food, and restaurants. Brand names include Pepsi-Cola, Slice, Mountain Dew, Frito-Lay, Taco Bell, Pizza Hut, and Kentucky Fried Chicken. Employees numbered 480,000 in 1997.

Elaine Franklin, manager of corporate information, wrote on May 16, 1996, to report that $1,000 invested in 1965 would have been worth about $90,000 in 1996, assuming reinvestment of dividends.

Although Coke and Pepsi are competitors worldwide, a much larger percentage of Coca-Cola earnings stem from outside the United States. Does this mean that Pepsi has more room to grow there?

20. Rockwell International Corp.

2201 Seal Beach Blvd.
PO Box 4250
Seal Beach, CA 90740–8250
NYSE symbol: ROK
IPO prior to WWII, date unavailable

Rockwell International Corp. researches, develops, and manufactures products for the aerospace, electronics, automotive, and graphics industries. It also produces factory automation equipment, fax and PC modem sets for trucks and automobiles, tactical weapons, spacecraft, and printing presses. Employees numbered 82,671 in 1997.

There has been a substantial shift in corporate activities since Donald R. Beall took over as CEO in 1988. He candidly answered my two questions:

All Rockwell businesses are expected to be a leader in their served markets (number 1 or 2).

We take the long-term view of our businesses and seek to maximize the potential of each. This is particularly true with respect to how we treat investments in capital and research and development.

Our financial goals are double digit growth in earnings per share, return on shareowners' equity in the 20% range and a strong cash flow to support investments, dividends, acquisitions, debt reduction, and as appropriate, stock repurchases.

Unfortunately, I don't have an answer to your second question. The original public offerings of the businesses that now make up Rockwell happened over many decades (some before WWII) and in many cases became part of a larger stream of publically owned equity before flowing into Rockwell. Consequently, developing the calculation you ask for would be a challenge, let alone arriving at an accurate number.

More recently, we have calculated that in the span of our 1995 fiscal year, the total investment return on Rockwell stock, including stock price appreciation and cash dividends was 41%.

21. Sara Lee Corp.

3 First National Plaza
Chicago, IL 60602–4260
NYSE symbol: SLE
IPO: 1946

Sara Lee Corp. is a superb marketer of consumer products worldwide; it manufactures brand-name food items, baked goods under the Sara Lee brand, household and personal care products like L'Eggs, Hanes, and Kiwi, and Hillshire Farms meat products. Employees numbered 149,000 in 1997.

Janet Bergman, V.P. of corporate affairs, answered my questions with justifiable pride on July 11, 1996. She pointed out that Sara Lee had ranked #1 or #2 in eight of the last ten *Fortune Magazine* surveys of the most diversified food companies. The board strongly encourages managers to act as if they own the business, reflecting the old Spanish proverb, "under the master's eye, the horse grows fat."

Sara Lee has over one hundred major brand names sold around the world. Six of these have sales of over $500 million per year, and twenty-five others have sales exceeding $100 million per year. Sara Lee does business in 150 countries around the world; 40% of its sales and 45% of its operating profits came from outside the United States in 1995. These percentages are double the international results of just ten years ago.

Sara Lee pursues multiple channels of distribution—with emphasis on the "direct to the consumer," for example, Sara Lee Bakery kiosks and Sara Lee Sandwich Shoppes. Direct sales of household products, handled by over 350,000 sales representatives, together with catalogs that reach 9.4 million households, accounted for more than $1 billion in 1995.

Sara Lee began trading on July 10, 1946—fifty years before Janet Bergman's letter to me. A $1,000 investment on that day would have grown to $85,292 in 1996. Cash dividends would have accounted for an additional $18,908. Something to remember: Great size doesn't mean there is no room left for further growth.

22. Sealed Air Corp.

Park 80 Plaza East
Saddlebrook, NJ 07663–5291
NYSE symbol: SEE
IPO: ?

Sealed Air Corp. manufacturers a host of protective packaging material systems: Instapak foam-in-place systems, Aircap and Polycap-Plus air cellular cushioning material, Mail Lite and Cell-Aire foam. Dri-Lor provides absorbent pads for use in the food industry for meats, fish, and poultry. It is impressive to see the amazing application of packaging solutions to the problems of modern living.

In 1982 T. J. Dermot Dunphy, president and CEO, said: "The greatest compliment that a company can pay its founders is to carry their tradition of creativity."

On September 13, 1996, Mary A. Coventry, V.P. for corporate development, wrote me: "In response to your question about how much $1,000 invested when Sealed Air Corporation went public is worth today, we do not have that information available. However, we can tell you that $1,000 invested in 1970, assuming all dividends were reinvested and reflecting all stock splits, would be worth $198,353.22 as of June 30, 1996."

23. Sysco Corp.

1390 Enclave Parkway
Houston, TX 77077–2099
NYSE symbol: 844
IPO: March 10, 1970

Sysco Corp. distributes food products throughout the United States to every type of institution—hotels, restaurants, hospitals, schools. Merchandise comes from all over the world and then is marketed under the Sysco brand name and other national trademarks. Employees numbered 28,100 in 1997.

John F. Woodhouse, chairman of the board, wrote a long and detailed letter on April 26, 1996, to answer my questions. First he acknowledged the genius of the founder, John F. Baugh, who conceived the company and served as its architect. Baugh got nine totally independent companies to join their talent and resources and to subjugate their individual differences for the good of the whole and formed Sysco in 1970. Mr. Woodhouse credits the second reason for success to the growth in the food service industry in the United States from $15 billion in 1970 to $135 billion in 1996.

Food service establishments demand precise, exacting service, and from the beginning it has been the objective of Sysco Corporation to provide exactly this type of service to support our customers' desires. Thirdly, Sysco has always sought to employ outstanding leaders in our industry. We have always tried to identify the most talented people, treat them fairly, and provide them with very generous rewards when they handle their responsibilities appropriately. Fourth, Sysco's dedication to permitting our operation to have a significant degree of autonomy has been instrumental in the organization's progress.

On March 10, 1970, the day that Sysco became a public company, one could have purchased 57 shares at $17.50 (the original offering price) with $1,000. If those 57 shares were held today (ignoring the dividends that have been paid over the 106 consecutive quarters), they would have been increased by seven stock dividends/splits and would now be 3,565 shares. At the current selling price of $33 a share, the original $1,000 investment would have a market value of $84,645."

Individual leadership makes the difference. Of course, a growth industry helps!

24. Trinity Industries

2525 Stemmons Freeway
Dallas, TX 75207–2401
NYSE symbol: TRN
IPO: October 2, 1958

Trinity Industries manufactures railcars and containers for liquified petroleum gas and fertilizers, heat transfer equipment, highway guardrails, barges, and tugboats.

Christine Stucker, vice president, wrote me on June 3, 1996, that Trinity's success could be attributed to: "a dedication to our core competency of steel fabrication, and the loyalty and dedication of our employees." She added: "On October 2, 1958 Trinity Steel Co. was traded over the counter for 3 $7/8$ per share. Therefore, an investment of $1,000 would have purchased 258 shares of stock. Taking into consideration price appreciation and stock splits, 258 shares would now be worth $175,903 (4,955 shares at $35.50 share). Dividends were $40,402. The total value of a $1,000 investment in October 2, 1958 would be worth $216,305 as of March 31, 1996."

25. Tyco International Ltd.

One Tyco Park
Exeter, NH 03883
NYSE symbol: TYC
IPO: 1966

Tyco has several core businesses: disposable and specialty products; fire protection; electrical/electronic components; educational and medical installations; and industries ranging from food to telecommunications. David P. Brownell, senior V.P., wrote me on April 22, 1996:

> The basic philosophy in the company is to stick with the basics. We have a very small corporate staff (approximately 40), strong operating managers in the divisions, and incentives throughout the organization based on increasing earnings and cash flow a minimum of 15% over the prior year. We reinvest in our businesses to keep them the lowest cost producers with the highest quality products in their respective industries. And we reinvest in our employees by providing sound employee health benefits, competitive retirement plans, and opportunities for them to constantly improve their skills through education and training.
>
> An investment of $1,000 in Tyco stock in 1966 would be valued at $77,654 at the end of March, 1996. That is an average return of approximately 16%.

Tyco growth comes from highly disciplined acquisitions and emphasizing market leadership. Keep your eye on management leadership.

ACKNOWLEDGMENTS

Finally, I've arrived at that part of the book most satisfying to the author, "Acknowledgments." It means the book is finished! Not that it can not be improved and expanded. New ideas always go on for years after a book is published. There comes a time, however, when you have to say "enough" and review the long road travelled. An opportunity to remember and acknowledge all the wonderful people who helped.

I am particularly grateful to the Presidents, Chairmen of the Board, and the financial officers of over one hundred of the most successful public corporations who were kind enough to be interviewed or answer my questions about the fantastic success of their corporation. Unfortunately, due to limited space, not all of them could be quoted in their entirety.

Thanks too to all the investment bankers, brokers, and attorneys who were part of my Wall Street experience. They provided much of my education in "street smarts."

Special recognition and appreciation to my wonderful family, Shelley, James, Joseph and Robert, writers and literary savants all, who read and encouraged my work in progress.

There was one person whose help was so extraordinary that I wanted to list his name on the cover of the book. My publisher, however, said, "It's *your* book—acknowledge his contribution in the appropriate section." He is Moss J. Plaine, M.B.A. and J.D., "broker supremo" with Burnham Securities, who acted as my eyes and ears, research analyst, computer guru and data bank for stories and anecdotes I had told him through the years.

Special thanks to Carol Plaine and Lynne Lumsden for their indulgent and insightful editorial guidance, and to Maria Eliades and Joan Lyden for deciphering and typing my holiographic script.